Economies of the World

EDITED BY

NITA WATTS

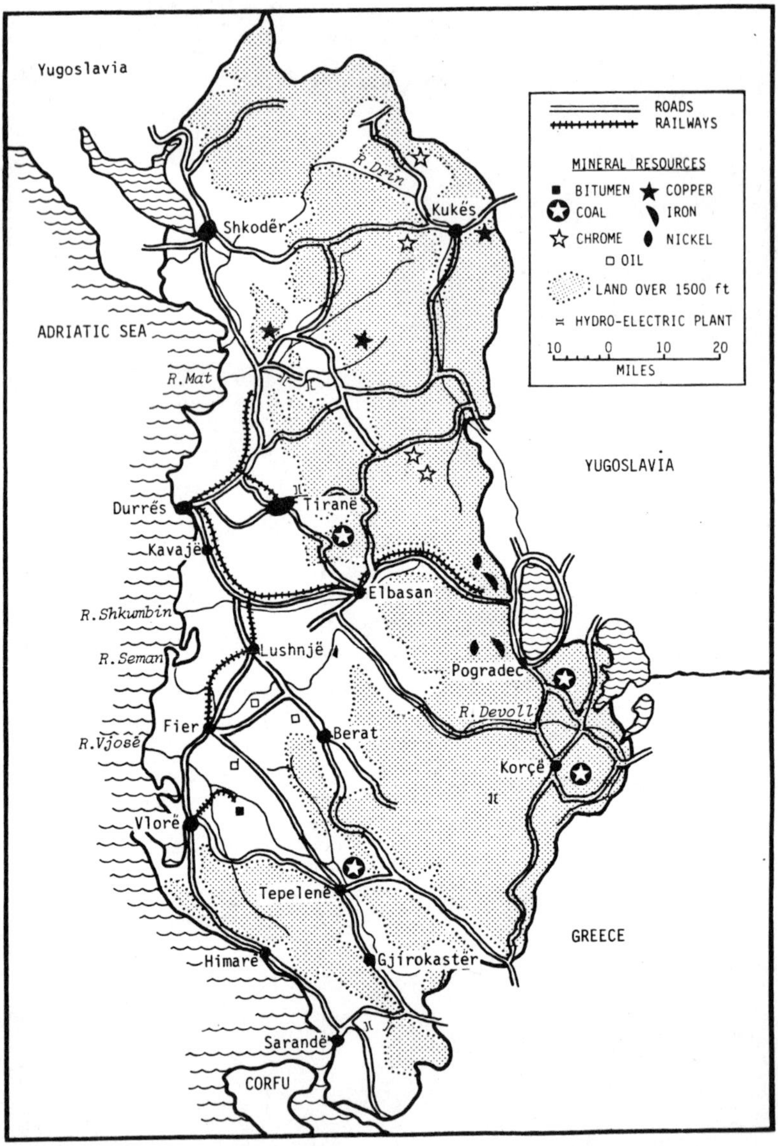
Yugoslavia
ROADS
RAILWAYS
MINERAL RESOURCES
BITUMEN
COPPER
COAL
IRON
CHROME
NICKEL
OIL
LAND OVER 1500 ft
HYDRO-ELECTRIC PLANT
10 0 10 20
MILES
R. Drin
Kukës
Shkodër
ADRIATIC SEA
R. Mat
YUGOSLAVIA
Durrës
Tiranë
Kavajë
Elbasan
R. Shkumbin
R. Seman
Lushnjë
Pogradec
R. Devoll
Fier
Berat
R. Vjosë
Korçë
Vlorë
Tepelenë
GREECE
Himarë
Gjirokastër
Sarandë
CORFU

Stalinist Economic Strategy in Practice

THE CASE OF ALBANIA

BY

ADI SCHNYTZER

OXFORD UNIVERSITY PRESS
1982

Oxford University Press, Walton Street, Oxford OX2 6DP
London Glasgow New York Toronto
Delhi Bombay Calcutta Madras Karachi
Kuala Lumpur Singapore Hong Kong Tokyo
Nairobi Dar es Salaam Cape Town
Melbourne Auckland
and associates in
Beirut Berlin Ibadan Mexico City Nicosia

Published in the United States by
Oxford University Press, New York

British Library Cataloguing in Publication Data

Schnytzer, Adi
Stalinist economic strategy in practice.
–(Economies of the world)
1. Albania–Economic Conditions
I. Title II. Series
330.94965'03 HC407.A/
ISBN 0–19–877125–8

Library of Congress Cataloging in Publication Data

Schnytzer, Adi.
Stalinist economic strategy in practice.
(Economies of the world)
Bibliography: p.
Includes index.
1. Albania–Economic conditions. 2. Communism –Albania. I. Title. II. Series.
HC402.S36 1982 338.9496'5 82–8040
ISBN 0–19–877125–8 AACR2

We would like to thank Victor Gollancz Ltd. for permission to reproduce the frontispiece map of Albania which is based on one drawn by Harry Hodgkinson for *The Albanians: Europe's Forgotten Survivors* by Anton Logoreci.

Set by Thames Typesetting, Abingdon
Printed in Great Britain at
The University Press, Oxford
by Eric Buckley
Printer to the University

For my father, teacher and master

ISRAEL SCHNYTZER

May his memory be for a blessing

PREFACE

This book discusses economic development in Albania between 1945 and 1977. Thus, the analysis proper ends in the last years of the Chinese presence in Albania. This timing has the advantage that, throughout this period, the Albanian government pursued a development strategy predicated on a steady stream of foreign aid.[1]

My thanks go to my thesis supervisor, Michael Kaser, for providing me with unstinting assistance and inspiration during my stay in Oxford. Thanks are also due to Nita Watts, the editor of this book, for her helpful comments, and to Stuart Mann who made my study of the Albanian language such a pleasure. The other scholars who have commented on various portions of the draft and tolerated my obsession with Albania are too many to name.

At the personal level, I would like to give my deepest thanks to my mother, Klara Schnytzer, who, together with my late father, Israel Schnytzer, provided me with an upbringing that encouraged learning and who financed my stay in Oxford. Greatest thanks are due to my wife, Judy, a woman of valour, who looked after me, put up with my many moods and pandered to all my eccentricities. Without her, the book might simply not have been written.

Oxford 1980

A. SCHNYTZER

CONTENTS

LIST OF TABLES

CHAPTER 1

THE ANALYTICAL AND HISTORICAL FRAMEWORK

At first sight the Albanian economy would seem to be an 'enigma shrouded in mystery', in that its economic policies are formulated in statements quite unlike those applied by governments elsewhere in Europe, and the government goes to extraordinary lengths to suppress both dissent from its policies and publication of their results. As examples of this suppression, one can cite the expulsion (and probably execution) of the full corpus of economic ministers in the autumn of 1975 and the relative failure to publish statistics (amplified in Appendix C).

In terms of levels of output, Albania has remained the least developed country in Europe throughout its modern history. Since the Second World War, however, the economy has been transformed by the rapid development of an industrial sector, which had contributed only 4.4 per cent to net material product in 1938 but which now accounts for well over half.

Table 1.1 shows the changes in a series of major economic indicators up to 1973. From the table it is clear that the Albanian economy has

TABLE 1.1 *Growth indices for the Albanian economy (1938=1)*

	1950	*1960*	*1970*	*1973*
Gross domestic material product	1.7	4.0	8.3	10.7
Global agricultural production	1.2	1.7	3.1	3.5
Global industrial production	4	25	64	86
Retail trade turnover	1.4	6	10	13
Population (millions)	1.20	1.60	2.14	2.30

Source: 30 vjet Shqiperi socialiste (Tirana, 1974), pp. 21, 56, 112, 177, 183.

sustained rapid economic growth since 1950.[1] Even agriculture, traditionally a problem sector in centrally planned economies, has managed comfortably to outstrip the rate of population growth. Given Albania's evidently successful economic performance since the Second World War, it is surprising that so little has been written on the country's economy by Western scholars.

Hence, it is necessary both to discern the economic strategy and to elucidate its application. In undertaking the first task, one comes to comprehend a concept of much wider application, since Albanian economic strategy represents a literal application of that set out in Stalin's last published work, *Economic Problems of Socialism in the USSR*. The formulations in the book were never implemented as policy in the USSR.

Therein, it is hoped, lies one of the novelties of this study. But its corollary is also of topical interest, in that, following a uniquely 'Stalinist' path, Albania has borrowed very little from China. Because China was Albania's only ally, and because Albania deferentially used Chinese-style terminology (from the Cultural Revolution downward), observers have all too readily assumed that the Albanian leadership was Maoist.[2] Indeed, pilgrimages of Western European Maoists (and a few exiles from Eastern Europe) fortified this belief. Xenophobia in China precluded their travel to Peking, and Tirana was a 'second best'. In fact, they were misled, and in retrospect the break with China in 1978 need not have been unexpected.

An analysis of Albanian economic development reveals that the establishment of a set of institutions that would facilitate rapid industrial growth has at times, not surprisingly, been subordinated to a desire on the part of the party leadership to remain in power.[3] In particular, it may be argued that the decentralization of economic decision-making power implied by the 1966 reorganization of the system of economic planning and management was inspired more by the need to quell popular unrest and enhance the party's influence throughout the economy than by any direct link between the old planning system and economic performance.

A discussion of the salient features of the Stalinist development strategy and its application to the Albanian economy throws light on some of the problems likely to be encountered in other small developing economies if an attempt is made to achieve high rates of growth of industrial output in the absence of a sufficiently large skilled workforce and at the expense of the agricultural sector of the economy.

The policies adopted by the Albanian government in its attempt to overcome two major constraints on industrial development are here analysed with a view to discovering the important points of interaction between the planning and management system and the industrialization strategy. Thus, Albania's enforced reliance on foreign aid is considered in the context of the use made of the monopoly of economic decision-making power within the policy, planning, and administrative hierarchy to channel foreign capital efficiently into priority branches of industry. A further area of interest is opened by the exploration of the place of aid in a programme ostensibly based on 'self-reliance', and this is discussed in the context of the debate on the 'two-gap problem'.

The second important constraint implied by the Stalinist development strategy arises from a conflict between the high rate of domestic saving necessary for its successful implementation and the need, if possible, to obtain the co-operation of the population in pursuing development goals, or at least to secure their acquiescence. An estimated index of per capita consumption is used (in Chapter 5) in conjunction with data on changes in the distribution of income to show that the Albanian leadership has been unwilling to implement policies that would reduce the real income of workers or peasants. Rather, it emerges that attempts have been made to forestall undesired increases in consumer demand by reducing – when expedient – the real incomes of managerial and administrative salary-earners. It will be argued that the power base necessary to prevent potentially dangerous opposition to such measures has been created partly through the institution of ideological campaigns and partly through schemes for worker participation and control within the economic planning system.

THE CLASSIC SOVIET MODEL

The classic Soviet model of economic administration has been the prototype for all socialist centrally planned economies, and its essential features provide a backdrop against which to view the Albanian implementation of a Stalinist development strategy.

According to Wlodziemierz Brus,[4] planning and management of the economy in the classic Soviet model is characterized by five major features, the last four being in some measure a consequence of the first.

(1) There is a concentration of practically all economic decisions on the central level (except for individual choice in the fields of consumption and employment). The most important of these decisions are those relating to such basic economic proportions as the rate of accumulation and the rate of investment, which in turn determine the growth rate; the distribution of investment funds between various sectors of the economy; the division of the consumption fund into collective and individual consumption; and the determination of the main proportions of current output in accordance with the adopted structure of income distribution.

(2) The nature of the plan is hierarchical and the links between different parts of the economic apparatus are vertical. Since the majority of economic decisions are taken centrally and economic plans are generally addressed to specific enterprises, the intermediate levels of the state hierarchy will be involved in considerable negotiations with both the central planners and enterprise management. But there is little in this system to encourage horizontal links between suppliers and customers.

(3) The imperative form of transmitting decisions is downwards. Lower levels of the hierarchy usually receive plan tasks as orders which must be obeyed regardless of the prevailing economic climate. Further, if the central authorities feel the need to make changes in a plan in mid-stream, the enterprises must alter their activities and fall in line with the revised plan. Material incentives are generally used to ensure compliance on the part of subordinates in this system; but, since the complex of plan targets given to the enterprise is often imperfectly co-ordinated, enterprise management is often faced with a set of alternative activities, all leading to material reward (or avoidance of penalty). Under these circumstances, it is not surprising that decisions taken at enterprise level sometimes conflict with, rather than promote, the goals of higher levels in the hierarchy.

(4) There is a predominance of economic calculation and planning in terms of physical units. From the viewpoint of central planners, planning in physical units clearly minimizes the risk that enterprises will carry out undesirable substitution in production. On the other hand, an unwillingness to use price as an aggregator in detailed plan formation implies ever-increasing plan complexity as the variety of goods produced in the economy increases.

(5) Money plays a passive role within the state sector. In the classic Soviet model, workers are paid in notes and coins and spend this active money in their capacity as consumers. Inter-firm transfers are, however, carried out according to plan. Since unplanned deliveries are illegal, an enterprise has no need of active money beyond the wage bill. On the other hand, the pricing of goods used within the state sector and the maintainance of transfer accounts provide the central authorities with a mechanism for checking the activities of enterprises. Thus, on receipt of a planned delivery, the enterprise pays – by cheque – an amount specified in the financial plan. This amount is credited to the supplier's account in the central bank. Ideally, therefore, the central bank should be able to alert the planners if plan violation is occuring at the base.

These are the five essential characteristics of the centralized planning system.[5] The ideological underpinnings of the system and its implementation and modification in Albania are considered in Chapter 2. It should be clear that a planning system in which most decisions are taken at the central level is well suited to the rapid mobilization of resources in key sectors of the economy. The complexity of the economic system demands that planners focus on priority sectors and treat the rest of the economy as a residual. This is in sharp contrast with the perfectly competitive market system, in which the forces of demand and supply ensure optimal 'planning' in all sectors but permit unpredictable changes in output mix. Even in a regulated market system, the central authorities' priorities can be assured only up to a certain point, beyond which central *direction* – with its concommitant weakening or suspension of the market – is required.

In the classic Soviet model of economic administration, the development of heavy industry has a higher priority than that of light industry, the output of producer goods is generally planned to grow more rapidly than that of consumer goods, while industrial development takes precedence over agricultural development. It is for this reason that the major emphasis in this book is on the development of Albanian industry. Albanian agriculture, while of considerable interest in itself, is treated – in accordance with Stalinist development strategy – as a residual. Chapter 3 considers the industrialization process in Albania.

The priority development of heavy industry requires the availability of certain scarce raw materials and technologies. The Soviet Union, being well endowed with minerals and sources of energy, was able to achieve this goal without placing undue strain on its balance of payments, though the persistent neglect of agriculture has led, in recent years, to considerable food import bills. Economic self-reliance – in the sense that growth targets may be met without running a balance of payments deficit – has been a long-term goal of the Albanian government since it took power in 1944. However, in no year since that time has this goal been reached. The impact of trade and aid on Albanian economic development is discussed in Chapter 4.

In the classic Soviet model, the high rate of domestic saving necessary for the rapid development of heavy industry implies a potential conflict with the need to provide incentives for the mass of workers to behave in ways that promote this goal; and in the Soviet Union rigid adherence to the priorities of the central authorities has in fact often resulted in temporary reductions in the real income of the population. As has already been indicated, the Albanian government's income distribution policy has aimed at avoiding, or at least 'defusing', this potential conflict.

THE ORIGINS OF STALINISM IN ALBANIA

It has been suggested above that the development strategy of the Party of Labour of Albania (PLA) is based largely on the guidelines set out by Stalin in *Economic Problems of Socialism in the USSR*. In this section an attempt is made to present those features of Albania's modern history that help to explain the close adherence of the PLA leadership to Stalinist ideology. First, evidence is presented to support the contention that the adoption of Stalinist ideology by the leadership of the PLA was voluntary, and not the result simply of subservience to the Soviet government. Second, it will be argued that the breakdown in Albanian–Yugoslav relations in 1948 partly explains the enduring attraction of the ideology. Finally, it will be argued that Albania's natural resource endowment, in any case, favoured the adoption of the Stalinist development strategy.

The history of the communist movement in Albania is not well documented. The official *History of the Party of Labour of Albania*[6] gives 1928 as the year in which cells were first set up in Albania, while Marmullaku[7] suggests that it was 1927. By 1940 there were three prominent communist groups in the country: the Korça, the Shkodra, and the 'Youth' group. The formation of these groups and the struggles between them need not be discussed here.[8] Suffice it to note that Albania's first link with the Soviet Union was provided by the formation of an Albanian Communist Group in Moscow in 1927. An important member of this group, Ali Kelmendi, returned to Albania in 1933 as the Comintern's representative and is reported to have exerted a strong influence on the organization and idelogical direction of the Korça group, from whose ranks the future leaders of the PLA were to emerge.

On the other hand, it cannot be assumed that the Korça group was to become a miniature of the Communist Party of the Soviet Union, for it also came under the influence of communists who had embraced Marxism in Western Europe. In view of the impact he has had on the development of Albanian economic ideology and the goals of the PLA, it may prove fruitful to provide a brief biography of the most important of these men, Enver Hoxha.

Hoxha was born on 16 October 1908 in Gjirokaster, of middle-class Muslim parentage. He completed his Albanian education at the Lycée Française in Korça and was awarded a government scholarship to study engineering at Montpellier in France. He soon joined the Communist Party of France, and, as a consequence, lost his scholarship. In 1934 he moved to Paris, where he wrote several articles for *L'Humanité* attacking Zog's subservience to the Italian government, and began to study Law. Hoxha's activities and his links with other Albanian communists in Paris, were eventually discovered by the Albanian government and he was forced to move to Belgium. In Brussels he continued to read law but, for reasons that are not known, did not complete his studies.

Hoxha returned to Albania in 1936 and joined the Korça Communist Group. Although he was not a leader of the group, his popularity among Albanian communists, which probably resulted from an astute decision not to become involved in the power struggles of the three communist groups, led to his election as the first head of the Provisional Central Committee of the Communist Party of Albania (CPA) in 1941. The Party had been founded as a coalition of the three groups at a four-day meeting which convened in Tirana on 8 November 1941. The resolution of the meeting makes clear the organizational and ideological direction in which the CPA was intended to develop:

The party should not be a party of the old type, a party similar to that of the Second Social-democrat International infested with decay, inactivity, nepotism, factionalism and betrayal of the interests of the working class. We want a party capable of leading the working class in battle to victory. . ..[9]

It was further argued that the party would have to purge itself of all Trotskyite and anarchist influence and set itself the following task: 'We should strive energetically to uplift the cadres ideologically, theoretically, and politically by imparting to them the Marxist–Leninist theory. . ..'

Thus, while it was hoped that the CPA's ideology would be Stalinist, the need – as late as this – to order the translation and publication in Albanian of such works as the *History of the CPSU (Bolsheviks), Short Course*, as well as a number of works by Marx, Engels, Lenin, and Stalin, throws doubt upon the extent of Kelmendi's influence on other communists up to that time. The hypothesis that Comintern influence in Albania was weak is further supported by an examination of the writings of Enver Hoxha during the Second World War. Thus, with respect to the role played by Britain and the United States during the war, the first edition of the organ of the CPA's Central Committee, *Zëri i popullit* (Voice of the People), published on 25 August 1942, noted

The three great allies are fighting today for one aim: *to crush fascism.* The Soviet Union, with the Red Army of workers and peasants headed by comrade Stalin, leads the way as the vanguard. Then come the two great democracies: Britain and America, two great powers with colossal economies, which are preparing for a Second Front in Europe.'[10]

Further, it was asserted that Albania could be liberated only from within:

Zëri i popullit will rally all the virile energies of the Albanian people, the energies of all those who have understood once and for all that,
'Freedom is won,
It is not donated'.[11]

Indeed, even towards the end of the war, there is evidence to suggest that Hoxha had not ruled out the possibility of good relations with the West in later years. In his speech at the October 1944 Berat Congress, Hoxha stated: 'The great allies, England and the United States of America, which with their hard and continuous bombardments were inflicting on Germany, internally as well as along the whole Western front, great damage, opened in France the lightening thrust. . ., a thrust which will expedite the liberation of Europe from Nazi Germany. . ..'[12] Then, in his speech before the April 1945 Youth Congress, Hoxha declared:

Think . . . what would have happened if the people of the Great Democracies, of Great Britain, were not strong, those people who placed in the service of the anti-facist war all their economic and military potential; if it were not for the great English and American Armies which stormed the German fortress from the West; if it were not, in the first place, for Churchill and his rare ability as a leader; if it were not for the great Roosevelt, whose death has grieved our people because we lost one of our great friends, and the progressive world one of the true defenders of democracy and freedom.[13]

Hoxha's seeming unwillingness to appear as an unquestioning supporter of the Soviet Union is not inconsistent with an earlier statement, made on the occasion of the arrival in Albania of Comintern directives in 1943. Hoxha noted that no previous directive had ever been carried out in Albania; 'the directives were sabotaged because they did not find favourable soil'.[14] The speech also provides evidence that Hoxha and his colleagues had been careful to treat incoming Soviet influence selectively. Thus, while several members of the Moscow Communist Group had returned to Albania, only one – the already deceased Ali Kelmendi – 'whose name all of us communists must hold in high regard, propagated the correct line of the Communist International. He, and only he, carried out his task as a communist pioneer should do'.[15]

Finally, it should be noted that when Hoxha's new government arrived in Tirana on 28 November 1944 it had seized power without the aid of any Red Army troops.

It would thus seem reasonable to argue that the attraction of Stalinist ideology to the CPA leadership – or, rather, to the supporters of Enver Hoxha in the leadership – stemmed more from the fact that no other formulation of Marxist ideology based on socialist practice was then in existence than on Soviet pressure on, or influence within, the CPA. However, this does not explain the enduring nature of Stalinism in Albania when other East European countries, who were provided with Stalinist leaders educated at the source, have long since revised their ideologies and development strategies. An analysis of the relations between Yugoslavia and Albania in the immediate postwar period lends support to the hypothesis that Hoxha became a lifetime Stalinist in 1949.

Although official Albanian histories fail to acknowledge the fact, two Yugoslav communists, Miladin Popovic and Dusan Mugosa, were present at the founding of the Albanian Communist Party. N.C. Pano has suggested that they acted on behalf of the regional committee for Kosovo-Metohija of the Yugoslav Communist Party, and that they were instrumental in bringing the three Albanian communist groups together. Regardless of the degree of accuracy of Pano's contention, it is clear that Yugoslav influence was exerted on the CPA from its very inauguration. Thus, the new Albanian Constitution, drawn up in mid-1945, 'was a virtual carbon of the Yugoslav Constitution of 1945, with the major exception that the federal structure of Yugoslavia was not adopted'.[16]

On the other hand, a part of the CPA leadership, led by Sejfulla Malëshova, desired that the Albanian government should pursue an independent line on foreign policy, maintaining good relations with the West. They also argued for an initial period of economic development within a capitalist framework and government by a popular front representing a wide variety of political opinion. Malëshova's opponents, chief among them Koçi Xoxe, saw that, if these policies were implemented, Yugoslav influence and the CPA's hold on the country would both be weakened. Hoxha's position in this factional struggle is unclear, but evidence cited above lends credance to Pano's view that Hoxha was probably sympathetic to Malëshova's position. None the less, he 'began to waver under pressure from the Yugoslavs and their spokesman in the Albanian Party, Xoxe. Realizing the weakness of his own position, he joined forces with the pro-Yugoslav clique at a meeting of the Politbureau which was held between December 6 and 11, and denounced the stand of Malëshova and the moderates.

Koçi Xoxe's position as Minister of the Interior and Party Organizational Secretary allowed him to initiate the purges of several pro-Malëshova and anti-Yugoslav members of the CPA in advance of the Sixth Plenum of the CPA Central Committee, which convened on 21 February 1946. At this plenum Hoxha again sided with Xoxe, and Malëshova was expelled from the Central Committee. The plenum also decided to increase the rate of nationalization and to carry out more radical agricultural reforms and agreed 'that Albanian foreign policy should be orientated towards the Soviet Union and the People's Democracies'. It was also announced that the CPA's First Congress would be held in May 1946.

In the spring of 1946 the People's Assembly elected a new cabinet.

Enver Hoxha was given the posts of Prime Minister, Foreign Minister, Defence Minister, and Commander-in-Chief of the Armed Forces, and continued to serve as Secretary-General of the CPA. Koçi Xoxe, on the other hand, remained Minister of the Interior and Party Organizational Secretary. That Hoxha saw Xoxe and the Yugoslavs as a threat to his leadership was made clear by his attempts to get rid of them. According to Pano,

His efforts, however, ended in failure. Xoxe and the Yugoslavs thwarted his plans to call the Party Congress scheduled for May, perhaps because they feared that this body might take an anti-Yugoslav stand. The Soviet government side-tracked his request to visit Moscow, and the Albanian Politbureau rebuffed his draft of a resolution condemning the policies of Yugoslavia in Albania during and after World War II.

His attempt temporarily thwarted, Hoxha submitted to Yugoslav pressure for closer ties between the two countries and signed a Treaty of Friendship, Co-operation, and Mutual Aid on 9 July 1946. The execution of the provisions of this pact would have effectively incorporated the Albanian economy into the Yugoslav Federation. It called for the establishment of an agency to co-ordinate the economic plans of the two countries, for the standardization of the two monetary systems, and for the creation of a common price system and a customs union. However, implementation of these measures did not proceed smoothly. In 1947 the Albanian government objected to the Yugoslav valuation of Albania's raw material exports, the method by which Albanian investment in joint companies would be calculated, the alleged failure of the Yugoslavs to contribute the agreed share of capital to the companies, and an apparent attempt made by a joint shipping company to control Albania's foreign trade. Complaints were also made that Yugoslav experts in Albania were 'sabotaging' the economy in an attempt to bring about a change in government.

In an effort to resolve these issues, the Albanian government sent Nako Spiru, Chairman of the State Planning Commission, to Belgrade. It was also part of Spiru's task to obtain the Yugoslav aid necessary for the fulfilment of the 1947 Nine-month Plan. The Yugoslav government stipulated that the aid would be forthcoming only if the joint commission to co-ordinate Yugoslav and Albanian plans was immediately set up. The Albanians refused to accept this arrangement. Spiru's main argument was that, if the two economies' plans were co-ordinated, the Albanian economy would remain backward and forever dependent on Yugoslavia. In the event, Pano argues, Tito's true objectives with respect to Albania were signalled when the Yugoslav government proposed to Spiru that a secret pact be signed between the two countries, ensuring the protection of Yugoslav interests in Albania in the event of any change in the CPA leadership. It may be that Belgrade was becoming aware of the extent of the support within the CPA for Hoxha's attempts to rid himself of Xoxe. In any event, Spiru refused to sign the pact, and his mission ended with Albanian–Yugoslav relations worse than they had been when he arrived in Belgrade.

Possibly as a consequence of the failed mission, Xoxe initiated new moves against his opponents in the CPA leadership. On 20 May 1947 the Albanian government announced that nine members of the People's Assembly with known anti-Yugoslav sentiments had been arrested, tried, and convicted of plotting against the state. Malëshova was among those purged in Xoxe's attempt to swing a majority of the leadership in his direction.

In June 1947 the Central Committee of the Yugoslav Communist Party accused Hoxha of pursuing an independent line domestically and in foreign policy, and of fostering anti-Yugoslav feelings among the Albanian population. However, the CPA Politbureau did not respond to this pressure in the way Xoxe wished. Rather, it denounced the Yugoslav statement as another attempt to interfere in the internal affairs of the CPA. This setback led to a change in Yugoslav tactics, and on 12 July 1947 the Yugoslav government announced that it would provide 2 billion dinars credit to help the Albanians fulfil the 1947 plan.

Even though Hoxha had the support of a majority within the CPA leadership, the inherent weakness of his position had become clear. Consequently, he turned again to the Soviet Union for assistance, and on this occasion Stalin invited him to Moscow without, according to Pano, informing the Yugoslavs. The Soviet Union offered to furnish Albania with aid for the development of light manufacturing industry, and Stalin's handling of the affair suggests that he was not in full agreement with Tito over Yugoslav policy towards Albania. Pano argues that Stalin was not ready to rebuke the Yugoslav leadership publicly in mid-1947 because it might have jeopardized the creation of the Cominform, since Tito had been assigned the task of laying the organizational groundwork for the new body.

Defying the wishes of Belgrade, the Hoxha faction of the CPA leadership initiated a new economic plan, which stressed the development of light industry and the mechanization of agriculture, and concluded a trade agreement with Bulgaria in August 1947. This was followed, in December of the same year, by the signing of a Treaty of Friendship, Co-operation, and Mutual Assistance with the Bulgarian government. Pano is probably correct in asserting that this act was carried out after consultations with Moscow and was designed to show that the Yugoslavs no longer enjoyed a privileged position in Albania. He notes that:

the Yugoslavs, through Xoxe, sought to have inserted in the treaty a clause which in effect stated that any joint action undertaken by Albania and Bulgaria should have prior Yugoslav approval. Although Xoxe in a midnight confrontation with Hoxha threatened to disrupt the ceremony at which the pact was to be signed, Hoxha remained firm and forced his pro-Yugoslav colleague to back down. During his stay in Sofia Hoxha also enraged the Yugoslavs by his failure to mention the name of Tito in public.

By the beginning of 1948, Stalin had apparently decided to set a trap for Tito in Albania. He informed Milovan Djilas that, contrary to the Soviet government's expression of disapproval, he, Stalin, had 'no objection to Yugoslavia's "swallowing" Albania, and that Moscow agreed with Belgrade that the "proletarian" Xoxe was far more preferable than the "westernized intellectual" Hoxha'. Partly in response to these reassurances, and perhaps out of a sense of desperation, Xoxe unleashed another attack on anti-Yugoslav elements in the CPA. In early 1948 the Central Committee of the Yugoslav Communist Party sent an emissary, Savo Zllatić, to Albania to assist Xoxe in the convocation of a Central Committee meeting intended finally to overthrow his opponents. The Eighth Plenum duly met on 26 February 1948, and its proceedings reflect the extent to which the Xoxe faction was nearly successful in ensuring a long-term Yugoslav presence in Albania. Hoxha was forced to perform self-criticism and join the condemnation of Spiru in order to maintain his post as Secretary-General. The Plenum expelled Spiru's widow, Liri Belishova (Spiru had commited suicide three months earlier) and demoted the Chief of the Albanian General Staff, Mehmet Shehu. It is probably significant that Shehu had spent 1945 and 1948 at the Voroshilov Military Academy in the Soviet Union. Although Pano argues that Shehu was opposed to a proposal to unify the Albanian and Yugoslav armies, his future close links with Enver Hoxha may be better explained by his postwar connection with the Soviet Union. The Eighth Plenum also approved Xoxe's proposals to merge the Albanian and Yugoslav economies and armed forces.

It thus seems reasonable to argue that, at this point, Enver Hoxha's position in the CPA, and possibly his life, could be saved only if the Soviet Union came to his aid. Fortuitously, a first step in the process was the expulsion of Yugoslavia from the Cominform, news of which was leaked on 28 June 1948. Albania was the first country in Eastern Europe to attack Yugoslavia; on 1 July all the economic agreements between the two countries were denounced and all Yugoslav experts were ordered to leave Albania within forty-eight hours. A ban was placed on the sale of Yugoslav literature in Albania, and the Albanian press launched a campaign of anti-Yugoslav propaganda which has continued, by and large, to this day.

It remained for Hoxha to eliminate his internal enemies and to find a replacement for Yugoslav aid. The latter aim he achieved in September 1948, when the Soviet Union concluded an economic agreement with Albania which effectively compensated for the loss of Yugoslav aid. At the Eleventh Plenum of the CPA Central Committee in the same month, Hoxha attacked Xoxe and his supporters, manoeuvred the reinstatement of Shehu and Belishova, and then announced that the long-awaited First Congress would take place in November of that year. The Plenum also decided to change the CPA's name to the Party of Labour of Albania (PLA).

It is interesting to note the leniency with which the Plenum treated the pro-Yugoslav faction. Xoxe retained his membership of the Politbureau and his post as Minister of the Interior; lost only his position as Organizational Secretary. But, while the reasons for this mild reaction are not known, events soon proved that it was to be only a temporary phenomenon. On 3 October, Xoxe lost the Interior Ministry to one of his supporters, Nesti Kerenexhi, while he took the post of Minister of Industry. Then, according to Pano, on 31 October,

the axe fell. Xoxe and his lieutenants, including Kerenexhi, were stripped of their government posts. Mehmet Shehu, who had previously been restored to his position as Chief of the Army General Staff, was appointed Minister of the Interior. This latter step was probably taken to gain the support of the army for Hoxha. The dictator was now preparing to deliver the *coup de grace* to Xoxe and his clique at the First Party Congress.

Hoxha called for Xoxe's expulsion from the PLA at the First Congress, which met from 8 to 22 November, and Xoxe was expelled. Hoxha also reappraised his view of the major factors influencing allied victory during the Second World War. He now argued that the party had been:

profoundly aware that the Soviet Union was bearing the brunt of the war, and seeing the manoeuvres of American and British reaction which during the war years, under its pseudo-democratic and anti-popular banner, sought to regroup reaction to weaken the Soviet Union, our Party and people hurled themselves with still greater courage and heroism into the war for the fulfilment of their dreams, regardless of the sacrifices, loyal to the end to the Soviet Union.[17]

Hoxha even suggested that all that the Albanian people had achieved during the war had been made possible because 'they did their duty... with the name of comrade Stalin on their lips'.[18] This modification in outlook indicates that Hoxha was well aware of the service that Stalin had performed for him. On the other hand, it cannot be concluded that Stalin's involvement in the affair was motivated by genuine feeling for either Hoxha or the Albanian people. Pano[19] is probably correct in asserting that Stalin's actions resulted from the Soviet leader's desire to prevent the formation of a pro-Yugoslav faction within the communist movement. Further, that Hoxha was not yet completely convinced of the advisability of following the Stalinist line in all matters is indicated by the (unsuccessful) secret overtures he made to the British and American governments to obtain diplomatic recognition for his government. Hoxha's conversion to the Stalinist cause probably became complete in March 1949, when he visited Moscow to sign a new trade agreement and Stalin gave him permission to proceed with the purge of Koçi Xoxe and his supporters. In May 1949 Xoxe and several others were tried on charges of treason and sentenced to be shot.

It seems reasonable to conclude that, while Enver Hoxha's early experiences in Western Europe led him to believe that Albania's post-war economic development might be made possible by an expansion of relations with both East and West, his near demise at the hands of Xoxe and the Yugoslavs ensured that Albania would in fact obtain most of its economic assistance from the Soviet Union. The remainder of this chapter is devoted to a brief discussion of economic development in Albania prior to 1945.

THE ECONOMIC BACKGROUND

When Albania gained independence in 1912 it was the poorest economy in Europe, and the onset of the First World War forestalled any attempt that might have been made to alter the situation quickly. Albania's position in the Balkans is reflected in the fact that per capita national income was a mere $40 in 1927 against $68 for Bulgaria, $77 for Yugoslavia, and $78 for Romania.[20] Almost 90 per cent of Albania's national income was derived from agriculture, and the backwardness of this sector is evidenced by the fact that only around 8 per cent of the land was under cultivation. On the other hand, 65 per cent of the value of Albanian exports in 1928 was comprised of livestock products.

In an attempt to foster economic growth successive governments attempted to obtain foreign aid. Albania first asked the League of Nations for assistance in 1922, without apparent success; and the Fan Noli government was similarly refused aid in 1924. When Ahmed

Zog came to power in 1925 he decided to rely on Italy for the much-needed help. The consequences of his decision were to play an important role in conditioning the PLA's approach to foreign aid questions after the Second World War, because Albania's economic dependence on Italy was soon accompanied by political dependence.

It seems reasonable to argue that Italy's motive as an aid donor was entirely selfish. Thus, the establishment of the Italian-dominated Albanian National Bank, as a consequence of a 1925 economic agreement, ensured the ready passage of profits made in Albania into the Italian economy. Italian companies were granted concessions to exploit Albania's natural resources, while the Italian government covered the Albanian balance of payments deficit; and this deficit was not insignificant – between 1926 and 1928 the value of imports totalled 103 million gold francs against exports of only 55 million.[21] Public works also came under Italian control with the formation, in 1926, of the Società per lo Sviluppo Economico dell' Albania.

In 1912 Albania had just seven roads, with a total length of 185 km, and the only substantial bridge was located at Shkodër.[22] During the First World War an additional 250 km was added to the network, but there was no further road construction until the Società built around 1,500 km between 1926 and 1939. The only hard-surfaced road in the country was that connecting Tirana with the port of Durrës. The projected railway between these two towns was only partly completed, but the port of Durrës was reconstructed, becoming one of the best ports on the Adriatic, and its primary purpose was to facilitate Albano–Italian trade. The port at Vlora was used for shipping bitumen and oil and had no cargo-handling equipment. Some idea of the slow rate of infrastructure development is suggested by the eight years taken to build the 13 km long Shrokë Canal. Much of the melioration work undertaken prior to the Second World War had to be repeated when the poorly constructed Kavaje Canal let in sea water to the marsh it had been intended to drain.

The Italian contribution to Albanian agriculture was not generous, and cultivation techniques remained primitive everywhere except at Sukth, the eventual site of Albania's first state farm. This area near Durrës was an Italian concession, being farmed by Italian colonists who were permitted to export their output direct to Italy without the payment of taxes. As one report has put it, 'this farm could hardly be considered part of the Albanian economy'.[23]

Zog's domestic policies also kept agricultural output at low levels. Thus, the agarian reform of 1930 provided for a limit of ownership of 40 hectares per owner plus 5 hectares for each wife and child, with larger farms being distributed among the tenants. Owners thus dispossessed would be compensated with shares in the agricultural bank. It seems that Zog's intention was to frighten wealthy beys who opposed him rather than to redistribute agricultural wealth; but the threat that the reform might be implemented militated against investment in the mechanization of large holdings. Since about a quarter of the agricultural area was owned by 3 per cent of farm households, Zog's manoeuvre put a significant brake on development. In 1938 there were just 32 tractors in the whole of Albania.

But the most seriously neglected sector of the Albanian economy before 1945 was manufacturing industry. By 1938 one substantial cement factory had been built in Shkodër; there were several cigarette manufacturing plants, a brewery, and several small plants for the production of soap, furniture, cardboard, handmade tools, and carts. The country's electricity needs were provided by 13 generators, and per capita output of electricity had not quite reached 9 kilowatt-hours by 1938.

Whereas the development of manufacturing industry in Albania was not seen as potentially beneficial to the Italian economy, the need for raw materials ensured that some attempt would be made to exploit Albania's considerable mineral wealth. The first concession to a foreign mining firm in Albania was granted in 1875 to an Englishman, who leased the bitumen mines at Selenice to an Italian company financed by the Banco di Santo Spirito of the Vatican. These mines have a long history, having been exploited in ancient Greece and the Roman Empire. In 1891 the concession was taken over by a French company, only to fall back into Italian hands in 1918, this time to the Società Italiana delle Miniere di Selenizza–Albania (SIMSA). Experts from Italy had already conducted exploratory drillings in Albania in 1913, when oil deposits were discovered, and the first successful oil well was drilled in 1918 by occupying Italians near Drashovicë, while Italian occupation forces also developed a coal mine near Tepelenë to obtain fuel for their warships.

After the war, competition from international companies began for mining concessions in Albania. Only parliamentary intervention in 1924 prevented the Anglo-Persian Oil Company from obtaining a monopoly of Albanian oil deposits. They did however receive about 25,000 acres near Kucovë. The remaining areas were divided among other foreign concerns, the most important of which was the Azienda Italiana Petroli Albania (AIPA). Throughout the 1920s, this Italian company gradually expanded its activities to such an extent that when, in 1932, AIPA bought the Anglo-Persian Oil Company's concession, it obtained a monopoly over Albanian oil. Meanwhile, SIMSA had expanded its activities to include copper mining at Pukë and Rrubiq, and another

Italian company, the Azienda Minerali Metallici Italiani, obtained a concession for the chromium mines in Pogradec, Kukës and Klos. By 1938, all of Albania's existing mines were being exploited by Italian companies.

One of the major factors influencing Mussolini's desire to control Albania's mineral wealth was his need for oil. A League of Nations sanction against Italy forced her to expand the output of Albanian oil, and between 1935 and 1938 output increased eighteen times to 108,000 tons; by 1942, the needs of the war effort had led to a doubling of this level of oil output. The Italian occupation of Albania in 1939 also facilitated the rapid development of other mining sectors. Chrome ore extraction increased seven times between 1938 and 1942, while copper output rose sharply and iron ore and manganese were mined for the first time. The German occupation (1943–4) resulted in the exploitation of natural gas, while coal output rose above its prewar level. Whereas production in all these areas was seriously interrupted towards the end of the war and much plant and equipment was damaged, there is no doubt that enemy occupation was beneficial to Albanian mining capacity.

However, the Second World War does not seem to have had any significant net effect on non-human resources in the rest of the economy. Thus, Italian plans for an extension of the area under cultivation were never carried out, though the introduction of new strains of grain did help to raise output. On the other hand, this gain in production was probably offset by the 33 per cent decrease in livestock numbers caused by their slaughter to feed both Germans and partisans. The net effect of the war on public works is difficult to assess. Under Italian occupation many new ashphalted roads and bridges were built, although by 1945 several roads had been damaged and forty-eight bridges destroyed. Finally, a comparison between 1938 and 1946 reveals that (in 1956 prices) mining output rose by 52 million leks and food processing by 960 million leks, whereas global industrial production rose by only 746 million leks.[24] The fall in output was greatest in wood and metalworking, electricity generation, and production of construction materials and manufactured consumer goods.

CONCLUSION

It seems reasonable to conclude that some of the difficulties encountered by the PLA in its attempt to industrialize the Albanian economy were the inevitable consequence of historically determined factors. Thus, it is possible to distinguish two contrasting aspects of the Italian presence in Albania. First, Albania's economic dependence on Italy had led to political dependence, in the manner predicted by Lenin's theory of imperialism, culminating in the occupation of 1939. This combination of personal experience and doctrinal conviction was sufficiently potent to ensure that a majority of the CPA would sense danger in Xoxe's flirtation with Yugoslavia. It was probably also an important factor in Albania's reaction to the Sino–Soviet dispute and – given that the PLA leadership has remained relatively stable – probably accounts in part for Tirana's anger with Peking over Tito's visit to China in 1977. On the other hand, the Italian mineral exploration, which revealed the extent of Albania's natural resource endowment, provided an early, and obvious, basis for the PLA's industrialization drive.

In other words, the political forces that led Hoxha to embrace Stalin might not have ensured reliance on the Stalinist development strategy if the raw material base, which might ultimately make an industrial Albania self-supporting, had not obviously existed. Thus, the PLA was to follow the Italian (as well as Soviet) example in expanding industrial output – although not exclusively mining – while neglecting the agricultural sector up to 1953. However, while Italian mining activities in Albania were insignificant in relation to aggregate Italian economic activity, and the necessity to import food into Albania to meet the needs of the urban population could have no significant impact on the Italian economy, the PLA's inability to supply its industrial sector on the basis of domestic agricultural production gave rise to a degree of economic instability which could be corrected only by a major, albeit temporary, switch in allocational priorities, which came at the end of 1953 (see Chapter 3).

It remains to explain the significance attached in this book to Stalin's *Economic Problems of Socialism in the USSR*. First, because it was Stalin's last major statement on economic development, it may be interpreted as the definitive summation of the Stalinist position on the economics of socialism. While the Soviet Union is mentioned in the title, Stalin leaves no doubt that he intended his ideas to be executed elsewhere also. Thus, referring to the textbook of political economy, the production of which his statement was intended to assist, he argues that the book is needed not only by Soviet youth, but 'particularly . . . by communists and communist sympathizers in all countries',[25] and he goes on to argue that communists abroad want 'to learn from us and to utilize our experience in their own countries'. On the other hand, it need not be assumed that Stalin's final statement is a reflection of Soviet practice; the crucial point is that *Economic Problems* provides a picture of Stalin's desiderata for the development of a socialist economy. In the remaining chapters of this book an attempt is made to evaluate the suitability of the Stalinist strategy for an economy that differs markedly from the Soviet economy, and it is argued that

Economic Problems in fact provides a reasonably clear and unambiguous development strategy.

CHAPTER 2

PLANNING AND MANAGEMENT IN THE ALBANIAN ECONOMY, 1945–1977

This chapter discusses the development of the Albanian system of economic planning and management in terms of attempts made by the PLA between 1945 and 1977 to establish a set of system rules that would yield desired economic results. It is argued that the PLA leadership has maintained three major goals throughout its period in power, and that the contemporary economic system is the direct product of attempts to reach these goals subject to various constraints. The three goals have been: to remain in power; to achieve the fastest possible rates of economic growth, particularly in industry; and to ensure that the PLA has the strongest possible direct influence on all detailed economic developments. Whereas the analysis in this chapter will attempt to evaluate the PLA's success in achieving the final goal, more consideration of the Albanian industrial development strategy is necessary before conclusions can be drawn about the extent to which the planning and management system has in fact supported rapid industrialization.

The retention of power obviously does not depend only on economic factors, but only these will be considered here. In this chapter attention is drawn to the schemes for worker participation and control that the PLA has introduced at various times in an attempt to increase popular support for the regime, and Chapter 5 comments on the way in which policies on consumption levels and the distribution of income have been related to the leadership's power base.

When the PLA came to power in Albania following the Second World War, a system of central planning had already been established by Stalin in the Soviet Union that might *a priori* have been expected to ensure far-reaching PLA influence over all details of economic development if instituted in Albania. The most succinct formulation of the ideology behind the Soviet planning system may be found in Stalin's *Economic Problems of Socialism in the USSR*, already mentioned above, and it will be argued that, to the extent that this ideology has not conflicted with other PLA goals, its guidelines have been adhered to in the development of the Albanian planning system.

THE IDEOLOGY OF PLANNING

The Stalinist position on the rules of a socialist economic system is based on two economic 'laws': the law of balanced, proportionate development, and the law of value. According to Stalin, the former law arose in a socialist economy 'in opposition to the law of competition and anarchy of production under capitalism'. The law's operation under socialism 'makes it *possible* for our planning bodies to plan social production correctly. But possibility must not be confused with actuality.'[1] By this, Stalin presumably means that the concentration of the means of production in the hands of the socialist state makes the non-market allocation of resources feasible; but, while arguing that planning is essential to a socialist economy, he has not defined the nature of the planning process in any detail.

Stalin's interpretation of the law of value and its role in a socialist economy yields more specific conclusions. Stalin, following Marx, defines commodity production as the production of goods for exchange between different owners. Thus, a product is a commodity only if it is sold rather than transformed within the same organization, and commodities exist under socialism only to the extent that different forms of ownership prevail. Consequently, all goods sold by state enterprises are commodities if they are bought by collective farms or private individuals. Stalin notes the corollary that it is possible for a good to be a commodity in some situations and not in others. This is the case when a machine is exported – thereby becoming a commodity – and another machine of the same type remains within the state sector of the economy – where it cannot be a commodity. The relevance of Stalin's discussion is that, where commodity production occurs, the law of value operates. In other words, individual responses to the forces of supply and demand govern the ultimate allocation of resources.

Within the state sector of a socialist economy, Stalin argues that the allocation of resources is not determined in this way since the sphere of action of the law of value is 'strictly limited and placed within definite bounds'.[2] It does, however, influence consumer goods production, and has wider influence to the extent that it 'trains our business executives to conduct production on rational lines and disciplines them'.[3] Stalin's limitations on commodity production in the state sector rule out the possibility of any extensive decentralization of economic decision-making to the enterprise level. On the other hand, a highly centralized economic system is not required, provided that decision-making power resides within the policy, planning, and administrative hierarchy. This implies options, which are exemplified by the changes in system rules adopted by the PLA in 1966 and discussed below.

THE ALBANIAN EXPERIENCE, 1945-1965

By the time the PLA came to power in Albania in 1945, the leadership had already decided on the introduction of a Stalinist system. There was to be central planning of the economy, with tight control over the operation of the law of value – that is, the role of commodity–money (market) relations – in the state sector. This point was forcefully made by Enver Hoxha in 1947 when addressing the People's Assembly:

The 1947 financial budget and the general state plan for 1947 will enable us to build a planned economy. We will be helped by the standardization of prices which allows us to plan state accumulation and does not leave the law of value to spontaneity, but guides the new structure and method of fixing and applying prices, and by the placing of wages and salaries on a correct basis; that is, he who works more and better gets higher pay when everything is taken into account: ability, work productivity, difficulties of the place of work, etc. All these will enable us to build the economy according to plan.[4]

The PLA intended to introduce the complete system of Soviet model plan indicators as soon as possible; but in fact they faced constraints which precluded the immediate establishment of so complex a system in Albania. First, the country had practically no industry to plan, and what did exist was spread thinly in small plants across the country. Second, the low level of education of the population meant that there were too few people adequately qualified to man a strong central bureaucracy. Finally, although the PLA leadership wanted a powerful state economic administration, it was already arguing that it must not act as an 'excessive or restrictive bureaucracy', and was suggesting that 'the broad masses should take part in it on a large scale'. The nature of this intended participation was not explained, but it was clear that the emphasis would be on the execution of planned tasks rather than on participation in economic decision-making:

Workers of Albania! . . . You are the greatest guarantee of our people's power. Exert all your efforts in carrying out the various tasks which face you in the factories and work-sites, in the state apparatus, or wherever you are employed. . . . You are working for your state power, for your people, for yourselves, so do your duty better than ever.[5]

Hoxha was probably already aware at this early stage that, since he came to power without strong Soviet backing (even if with Soviet goodwill) and was not willing to tolerate a Yugoslav presence in Albania, his survival as PLA chief would be possible only if he used his initial popular support as leader of Albania's liberating army to consolidate his power base. To this extent it might have proved imprudent to attempt to restructure rapidly a society recently ravaged by war. The measures actually taken to establish the classic Soviet model in Albania may be summarized as follows.

Nationalization of all public utilities and foreign-owned capital was the first step. This was completed in 1946 and was followed in the same year by the nationalization of domestically owned means of production and foreign trade; by early 1947 what little there was of Albanian industry was in the hands of the state. These measures allowed the State Planning Commission – which had been given its autonomy from the Economic Council, and made directly subordinate to the Council of Ministers, a year earlier – to draw up the country's first national plan, the nine-month plan of April–December 1947. This plan is reported to have been relatively simple in the sense that it covered only the manufacturing, mining, and agricultural sectors of the economy and that output targets for only a small number of goods were detailed in the plan. These targets were given in physical rather than monetary terms, and global indicators such as total industrial production or its rate of growth were not specified.

At the enterprise level, 1947 saw the introduction of the Soviet autonomous accounting system *khozraschet*. Having instituted this 'system', the Albanian planners were able to draw up a more sophisticated plan for 1948 than had previously been possible. Whereas the 1947 production plan was made up of selected output targets in physical units, the new plan provided more detailed specifications for the enterprise, material balances and norms of input utilization being used in plan formation for the first time. In 1947 investment had been undertaken on an *ad hoc* basis, whereas in 1948 the attempt was made to plan capital investment for projects ranked according to planner's preferences. In addition to the more complex planning of 1948, the Albanian government introduced various organizational practices borrowed from the Soviet Union, the most important being the socialist emulation campaigns. At the same time, it was drafting a five-year plan; but because of the conflict with Yugoslavia this was not implemented, and it was not until 1951 that the First Five-year Plan was launched. This was drawn up essentially in the form of material balances for a limited number of commodities and until 1956 planning remained at this simple level.

However, contrary to the party's stated aims, the state administration expanded very rapidly – so much so that by 1953 'such an apparatus weighed heavily on the people's economy, weakened its management and opened the road to bureaucracy'.[6] This led in the same year to a scaling-down of the state administration and the staff of mass organizations by 30 per cent, those losing their jobs being transferred to industrial and farm work. While the official reason given for this move may have some validity, it should be noted that similar changes took place elsewhere in Eastern Europe at the same time, implying that Soviet policy may have been an important factor. Further, it is possible that the PLA wished to remove politically undesirable people from the hierarchy, simultaneously providing industry and agriculture with additional workers.

In 1956 a money balance of household incomes and expenditures was calculated and national product by origin was computed. The intensity of planning in Albania during the Second Five-year plan (1955–60) was raised annually, until by 1959 the complete Soviet system of plan indicators had been adopted. Planning during this five-year period was also changed – at least in principle – with respect to the timing of plan publication. During the First Five-year Plan, annual plans had always been approved during the plan year. This meant that enterprises were forced to begin their annual operations on the basis of only the less detailed five-year plan indicators, whereas from 1956 onwards annual plans were to be made available before the beginning of the plan year. But as elsewhere in Eastern Europe, this has rarely been achieved in fact.

The internal organization of industrial enterprises was as highly centralized as the total economy, based as it was on the concept of 'one-man leadership' (*udhëqje unike*); and in terms of the Chinese notions of 'expertness' and 'redness', 'expertness' reigned supreme. However, economic decision-making power did not rest with the enterprise director, who was completely under the control of the relevant ministry or the Executive Committee of the People's Council of his district (*rreth*). Worker's interests were supposedly in the care of the Trade Union organs, while the primary party organizations were responsible for the ideological and political education of the working class. The rights of the trade unions in 1959 were as follows:

(1) to represent workers and employees, defending their interests, before all state organs and social organizations, on problems relating to relationships and conditions of work and the lives of workers and employees:
(2) to make proposals and take part in the preparation of draft-laws and other juridical dispositions linked to problems of production, wages, the lives and culture of workers, the defence of work, and other problems;
(3) to make and approve collective contracts and to control their execution; to take part in socialist emulation and evaluate its outcomes;
(4) to direct state social security; (etc.)[7]

It should be noted that neither the death of Stalin nor his denunciation by Khrushchev in 1956 had any immediate effect on the practice of economic planning in Albania. The position of the worker in the Albanian economy remained, until 1965, as it was in 1959. The worker was given no effective part to play in enterprise decision-making, and could only rely on the trade union organization to protect his material interests. Neither was there any significant change in the overall spread of decision-making power in the economy, the shift in allegiance from the Soviet bloc to China having had no apparent impact on Albanian thinking in this context.

But by 1965 it had become clear that the Albanian leadership was not satisfied with the results of the working of the economic system. The Third Five-year Plan target for global industrial production was 97 per cent fulfilled[8] and, taking into account the economic difficulties caused by the Soviet Union's economic embargo (following the conflict between the Soviet and Albanian party leaderships and the break in relations in 1961), it might have seemed that the industrial sector of the Albanian economy had performed well over the1961–5 period. However, following the split with the Soviet Union there had been a drastic downward revision of plan targets, and, as the discussion in Chapter 4 shows, other sectors of the economy had faired less well than industry. Thus, though in admittedly difficult circumstances, the classical Soviet model of economic administration was not producing economic growth rates to satisfy the leadership. It has also been suggested that economic failures were 'a major factor in triggering off the unrest that began to spread through Albania during 1965 and 1966'.[9] In other words, Enver Hoxha's position as leader of the PLA was in jeopardy; and this, probably more than any other factor, indicated the need for change.

The existence of various bureaucratic dysfunctions in the state apparatus, notably 'excessive memos, unnecessary reports, and countless documents', was noted in the Albanian press in 1965. An unsigned article in the organ of the Central Committee of the PLA, *Zëri i popullit*, gives a detailed breakdown of the paperwork being done by the Executive Committee of the People's Council in Durrës district. It points out that not only are unsolicited reports prepared for higher authorities and for enterprises, but that thc recipients of these reports often request information that they have already received from other sources; moreover, the staff of the Executive Committee had an excessive propensity to issue memoranda:

> To illustrate this it suffices to mention the fact that in nine months the Executive Committee of the People's Council of Durrës district filed 7,246 official memos (not counting petitions) and issued 5,783 memos (not counting copies) – a total of 13,029 memos! This number shows the nature of the existing bureaucracy.[10]

Finally, the article hints at disguised unemployment in the state sector of the Albanian economy. When asked why the Ministry of Agriculture continually requested useless information, 'after a slight hesitation an old specialist said, "If one abolished unnecessary forms, many employees of the Ministry would be idle".'

There is also evidence that the administration of enterprises was rather inefficient, absenteeism being very high: for example;

absenteeism without reason in 1963 in Durrës Port amounted to 8.8 per cent of work time. By September 1965, that is, during an eight month period, the economic enterprises in Durrës district had lost more than 40,000 days of enterprise work potential. In counting the number of days lost, we estimate a loss of 100 workers per day whose production, had they worked, would have been valued at more than 8 million new leks. It is obvious that the loss of work hours in some enterprises has resulted in an increase in wages, and as a result, an increase in costs.[11]

Although this is not said, the increases presumably refer to wages and costs per unit of output, the implication being either that workers are paid even when they do not report to work regularly, or that spasmodic absenteeism results in higher levels of employment – and of under-employment at certain times – than would otherwise be necessary. It seems reasonable to suggest that the extent of absenteeism in Albanian enterprises was one of the factors influencing the government to increase party and trade union influence at the shopfloor level in late 1965.

The poor quality of output and inefficient utilization of inputs were also criticized; and, finally, the method of evaluating enterprise performance came under fire. First, it was argued that, while global indicators such as the total volume of production were useful in expressing the 'dynamics of development', enterprise performance should be evaluated on the basis of more detailed indicators such as output mix and quality of products. The second criticism involved the use of labour productivity measured in value terms as an indicator of plan fulfilment. It was argued that using this indicator led enterprises to produce only those goods with relatively high prices and high capital requirements per unit. But it should be noted that this criticism is directed at the notion of the price system allocating resources, rather than at defects in the existing set of prices.

THE BACKGROUND TO SYSTEMIC CHANGE

The first signs that system rules would be changed appeared early in 1965 in press reports exhorting trade union organizations to do more educational work with the masses, not only in the form of lectures and conferences, but also at the work-bench. It was further argued that praise, as well as criticism, was necessary to raise the morale of the workers. The work of enterprise directors was criticized, and it was suggested that they were not explaining directives to the workers; it was also argued that a director must be a 'partyist' strictly following the 'party line'.

In October 1965 the PLA took a further step, apparently attempting to reduce popular unrest, when its Central Committee, in conjunction with the Council of Ministers, issued a call to the masses to participate in drawing up the Fourth Five-year Plan. In this so-called *Appeal*, it was explained that Albania was surrounded by 'imperialist and revisionist enemies' and was being subjected to an 'economic blockade', and therefore would have to build socialism relying on its own resources. It seemed clear to the leadership that, since the workers of Albania best knew their own capabilities and, probably, the capacities of their enterprises, it was going to be possible to draw up a 'just, real, mobilizing, and revolutionary' plan only if the workers were involved. It was argued that investments and construction projects should be 'more profitable, timely, and essential'. Workers were exhorted to approve plans that minimized expenses and waste, and party members were reminded that their duty was to further the 'ideo-political' education of the workers. The only specific change in planning methods introduced in the *Appeal* was that henceforth workers in enterprises would discuss broad plan targets, which the enterprise would use in drafting a detailed project plan, rather than being sent a detailed plan from the state hierarchy without any such preliminary. However, decentralization of real economic decision-making to the enterprise was apparently not contemplated.

According to the official history of the PLA, the discussions were a resounding success:

Responding to the call of the Party, the masses of the people discussed the indices of the Fourth Five-year Plan in such a lively and creative manner, with such a profound and revolutionary sense of responsibility as never before. In the plan they proposed to the Party and government, numerous indices exceeded even the most optimistic produced by state and economic organs.[12]

The precise nature of these discussions and the real extent of worker participation in them is difficult to gauge. An article in *Zëri i popullit*, reporting on the 1 November 1965 plenum of the Central Council of Albanian Trade Unions, quotes the situation in the Stalin Textile Combine as an example of a good approach to the planning problem:

The combine management and the trade union committee there bring out the key problems which determine the successful realization of the duties of the plan. The administrations of factories examine the technical–economic indices down to each worker and machine; they extract the results achieved by the best workers; and these, along with the propagandistic work for illuminating the political and economic importance of tasks, are placed in discussion in the brigades, complexes, shifts, and departments. In such an atmosphere of active, concrete, and responsible work, the workers give their highly valuable ideas not only about advancing the index of the plan, but also about steps for the successful completion of it. During the discussion of the pilot plan for 1966, 613 workers spoke here. Such efforts have had an influence on the increase of the mobilization of all workers for fulfilling their tasks.[13]

By contrast, the draft proposals for the 1966 plan in the Shkodër district were presented to the workers by enterprise management as a *fait accompli*, trade union officials often being absent from the meetings. This situation, the Plenum emphasized, should not occur in the discussions of the Fourth Five-year Plan. The emphasis in the changed approach to planning is clearly laid on greater propaganda efforts by the trade unions, and it is suggested that discussions in small groups – even down to brigade level – would prove more useful than large meetings: 'Study on a group basis, as well as the separate discussion of the production or service plan, of labour productivity, of the capacity of the machinery, of standards of use of materials, etc., would be more effective.'[14] Finally, the Plenum argued that only by bringing workers fully into the planning discussions could enterprise managers be prevented from drawing up minimum production plans with inflated resource requests.

It is reasonable to conclude that, under this participatory scheme, the Albanian worker was definitely not able to determine plan indicators solely on the basis of his own goals. But neither was he any longer to be simply the recipient of centrally determined tasks requiring unquestioning execution. The true position lies somewhere between these two extremes, and its elucidation provides an insight into the psychology of Albanian socialism. First, however, three concepts must be defined in the context of their use by the PLA: 'democratic centralism', 'class struggle', and the 'mass line'.

THE IDEOLOGY OF WORKER PARTICIPATION

Democratic centralism is a system of decision-making in which all matters are discussed at all levels of the relevant hierarchy prior to a decision being taken. This is the 'democratic' aspect of the process.

The decision is finally taken at some predetermined level of the hierarchy – generally near the top – and thereafter is binding on all members of the hierarchy. In Albania, democratic centralism is the major means of organizing the party and state hierarchies. Hence, workers' resolutions on the plan – if completely unconstrained – would still be susceptible to considerable change as the discussions continue up the hierarchy to the central planners. But, as will be seen from the discussion of 'class struggle' and 'mass line', workers' discussions must be far from unconstrained.

For the Albanian leadership, the 'class struggle' is waged on two fronts: foreign and domestic. On the foreign front since 1961, the struggle has taken the form of a continuous polemic against the United States and the Soviet Union, the latter being accused of imperialism, and a return to capitalism. The Albanian leadership argues that Soviet attempts at world hegemony in partnership with the United States is a betrayal of Marxism–Leninism. Further, in subjecting the members of Comecon to its will, the Soviet leadership has been responsible for a return to capitalism in those countries. The Albanians, therefore, have thought until recently that it was crucial that the only foreign influence permitted from abroad should come from China, whose government was allegedly equally anti-hegemonistic, conducting foreign affairs on the basis of 'proletarian internationalism'. On the home front, the 'class struggle' implies the purging of all remnants of the old bourgeois and feudal orders; that is, insistence that all members of society channel their thoughts and actions to the party's interpretation of Marxism–Leninism. The implications of this for the workers' plan discussions are clear. Targets and indicators suggested for incorporation in the plan must be more demanding of the enterprises than they would be in the absence of the class struggle. That this happens in practice is to be ensured by the trade union and party cadres who lead the discussion.

The third concept, 'mass line', ties in closely with the 'class struggle' in that the presence of the latter requires a strong – indeed, monolithic – party and state structure carrying out its tasks in accordance with Marxism–Leninism. But the ruling party – according to this doctrine – is the vanguard of the working class, and thus, by definition, applies the 'mass line' in its work. If any measures adopted by the government are not seen as correct by a worker, it is because he is still under the influence of ideologies belonging to classes other than his own.

Thus, it is reasonable to assume that the workers are highly constrained in their attempts to affect the planning of the Albanian economy. The discussion thus far might seem to be applicable to the situation in the Soviet Union under Stalin's leadership. There is however, a difference between the approach to planning in Stalin's Soviet Union and in post-1965 Albania, and it is one of psychology. The Albanian press has gone to some lengths to explain that great emphasis is placed on the use of persuasion and discussion rather than coercion, so that the workers should perceive themselves as being influential in plan formation. The Maoist experience has undoubtedly influenced this alleged difference in the approach of the PLA.

The role of trade unions as communist educators was enhanced in December 1965, when changes were made in the Labour Code relieving the trade unions of their functions in the administration of social security and pensions. These functions were now to be carried out by the State Committee for Labour and Wages, which would be unlikely to deal with worker's demands as sympathetically as would the trade unions.

Implicit in the November 1965 Plenum's argument that worker participation would constrain management is the assertion that, notwithstanding – and perhaps as a consequence of – the highly centralized nature of the classic Soviet model, it is not possible to ensure congruence between the goals of enterprise management and of the hierarchy. Thus, the greater involvement of workers in plan discussions may be seen as an attempt to supplement hierarchical pressure from above on directors with party-led pressure from below; and the plausibility of this hypothesis is reinforced by the ideological measures introduced since 1966 (see below).

The second series of changes in system rules involved the shift, in the middle of 1965, of artisan cooperatives and several enterprises from ministerial to local district control. While the majority of plan indicators still required the Council of Ministers' approval at this time, the partitioning of the hierarchy prepared the way for the decentralization of economic decision-making power that was to follow early in 1966. That changes in planning methods were to take place was implied by an article (unsigned, and thus suggesting possible authorship of a high-ranking official of the PLA) in the January 1966 issue of the organ of the State Planning Commission, *Ekonomia popullore*. This stressed the need to improve the management of the economy and the close relationship between economic and political factors in determining necessary management changes:

> The new duties to build the material and technical base of socialism represented by the rapid development of the forces of production, the international situation, and the political and economic conditions of the country demand a radical improvement in the management of the people's economy as a whole and its planning in particular.

It also suggested that the implementation by workers of the *Appeal* has indicated the type of changes required in the economy:

The further development of the drive and initiative of the working masses and the activities of state and economic organs at the centre, based on the Leninist principle of democratic centralism and its application in accordance with new tasks which may arise, makes it necessary to expand the authority and rights of these organs in regard to the management and planning of the people's economy. This problem is organically linked with the simplification and perfecting of the methodology of planning by avoiding unnecessary excesses and improving the categorization of the indicators approved by the various state organs.[15]

The article attributed the highly centralized nature of the planning system to the need for maximum mobilization of the country's resources during the Third Five-year Plan, when the Soviet Union's economic blockade first came into force. While conceding that the planning system was successful in this respect, it noted that centralization had given rise to harmful side-effects such as 'formalism and bureaucracy'. Further, so centralized had the system become that enterprises were often given plans that they had not even had a chance to discuss in draft form.

THE NEW SYSTEM 1966

It is not surprising that most of the changes recommended in the article just mentioned were soon made.

Decision No. 15 of the Council of Ministers, dated 17-21 February 1966 'On the Fundamental Principles of the Methodology of Planning', outlined the changes in the Albanian planning system intended for the period of the Fourth Five-year Plan, 1966–70. Although the *Decision* does not appear to have been published, its contents are discussed in detail by the Albanian economist, A. Backa, who begins with a definition of the planning methodology as 'the general criteria and special instructions concerning the drafting of the plans for each activity, the special indicators, the nomenclature of indicators and the examples of preliminary plans at all levels, the route of planning and the schedules, broadly employing the averaging and balancing methods'.[16] After giving an outline of the development of planning methods in Albania, he points out that the *Appeal* had revealed the need to revolutionize the planning system, and describes the projected changes.

The *Decision* is prefaced with four general points concerning the functioning of the Albanian economy. The first is that 'party spirit' (*partishmëria*) must apply in planning. Thus, unless the party line is maintained throughout, there is danger that the fundamental economic laws of socialism will be violated. 'Party spirit' is also said to imply that domestic and international political circumstances must be taken into account in planning, though the practical implications of this statement are not made clear. The second point reiterates Stalin's argument that the law of proportional development requires that the economy be planned. More specifically, it is noted that the rapid development of the economy and its sectors is possible only if the interdependencies between the different sectors are fully understood, and therefore Albanian economists are urged to make a thorough study of the economic system and its laws. The third point argues that workers must participate in planning since they are the people who actually carry out the plans and therefore know if there are 'hidden reserves' present. Without the incorporation of these reserves into plans, the plans cannot be 'real, mobilizing and revolutionary'. Finally, the economic blockade against Albania by the Soviet Union is mentioned again; its major consequence is that 'in drafting plans it is necessary that we start with the conditions of our country and rely mainly on our own forces'.

There were three major steps in the system of plan formation operative between 1949 and 1966. In March of the pre-plan year a draft of the plan was sent from the centre to the enterprises (the 'quota phase'). The enterprises then sent their revisions back to the centre (the 'preliminary plan phase') so that the State Planning Commission could co-ordinate the various plans and pass the final version on to the Council of Ministers for approval by 15 November. The final approved plan was then sent back to the enterprise as law. In addition to this procedure, import and export plans were drawn up separately in June of the pre-plan year and revised (to co-ordinate with the state plan) in November. Finally, in the old system quotas for imports and construction project outlays were set annually.

The new methodology simplified these procedures considerably. The quota phase of plan formation was eliminated and the remaining two stages were rescheduled; in June national enterprises, and in July Executive Committees of *rreth* (district) People's Councils, would send their preliminary draft plans to the relevant central organ (the Executive Committees' plans relating to small enterprises whose products are of predominantly local importance, and have no planning sections of their own). Upon receipt of the preliminary plans, the various central organs would process and co-ordinate their respective plans and send them to the State Planning Commission in August. During September the state plan was to be drawn up as part of the general planning procedure, figures from the Five-year Plan being used as guides to imports and to outlays on construction projects, replacing the previous annual quota system.

In addition to these changes in scheduling, the *Decision* drastically altered the plan indicator system. There was a significant reduction in the number of indicators in the state plan, so that only those considered essential for determining the main directions of economic and cultural development were included. Thus, whereas prior to the change the plan contained 550 indicators relating to industrial production that had to be approved by the Council of Ministers, the number of such indicators now dropped to 77. Unfortunately, the precise nature of these indicators is not known. Similar changes took place for all sectors of the economy; for agriculture the number fell from 320 to 42, and for investment and construction 100 items now required approval by the Council of Ministers instead of 500. One specific change that had important repercussions was the removal of the banking system's control over investments.

These reductions in plan indicators were accomplished by decentralizing the power to make many decisions that the Council of Ministers had previously taken. The recipients of the new powers were the ministries and the Executive Committees of the *rreth* People's Councils. In industrial planning, targets for major products would now be presented to the Council of Ministers only in aggregate, whereas before the change these targets were presented for each enterprise along with other indicators (now eliminated) such as a number of secondary products, products of local importance, technical and economic indicators for various branches, tasks for new product output, scientific research projects, projects for the mechanization of labour, and other improvements in technology.

In the trade sector, the distribution and material-and-technical plans were combined, only the index number for total sales requiring approval by the Council of Ministers. Similar aggregation occurred in labour planning, the Council of Ministers approving only the projected totals of administrative workers and their wages, and productivity indices for industry and construction. Finally, the Council of Ministers would approve plans annually whereas previously this had been done quarterly.

These simplifications of the plan sent to the Council of Ministers for approval did not, however, imply a simplification of the plan itself. The enterprises were required to draw up plans that were as detailed as before the change: the difference lay in the level of the hierarchy made responsible for dealing with the particular issues. The relative positions of the ministries *vis à vis* the Executive Committees would appear to be that generally the ministries received more power with respect to plan formation whereas the Executive Committees were expected to become more involved in ensuring plan implementation. Thus, under the old system the detailed plans, by *rreth*, for all production of national importance – transport, trade, investment and construction, education, culture and health – were approved by the Council of Ministers. The *rreth* plans for supply, distribution of local products, the workforce, productivity, wages, costs, and a number of other technical and economic indicators were the responsibility of the relevant ministry. According to the *Decision*, the detailing of all the above-mentioned plans would now be done by ministries and sent to the relevant Executive Committees to co-ordinate and supervise implementation.

The final type of change made by the *Decision* was in the method of evaluating enterprise performance. On this point, however, Backa is unclear. He states that global indicators such as the total value of output would no longer be the primary criteria for evaluation, arguing that enterprises and ministries would together be responsible for the fulfilment of plans in quantity and quality. The change in the structure of incentives accompanying the new planning system is discussed in detail in a later chapter; suffice it to note here that material incentives did not predominate.

By 1966 several other socialist economies had already attempted reforms of their economic mechanisms. Everywhere there was some decentralization of decision-making power, and everywhere, except in China, it had apparently been decided that the answer to their problems lay partly in greater freedom for decision-making by enterprises. Indeed, even in China that fraction of the Communist Party then in command of economic policy – later be labelled by Mao Tse-tung as the 'capitalist roaders' – had come to the same conclusion. Outside Albania, only the so-called 'socialist roaders' of the Chinese Communist Party maintained that significant decentralization within the state hierarchy (stopping short of the enterprise) combined with increased party activity at the local level was a successful means of building socialism.

It is therefore important to consider in greater detail the possible reasons for Albania's choice of this variant in the summer of 1965. In the first place, as has already been mentioned, Albanian economic ideology – being strictly Stalinist – demanded the rejection of an expanded role for the law of value in industry. Further, the weakening of the 'class struggle' would have left Albanian criticism of the Soviet Union without a *raison d'etre*, and this, at a time of improving Soviet–American and Soviet–Yugoslav relations, was unacceptable. Second, the Albanian economy was still the simplest in Eastern Europe, and the problems of information flow besetting the classic Soviet model in a more complex economy were unlikely yet to require the introduction of significant market or near-market relations into the Albanian state sector for their solution. Third, the problem of the regime's estrangement from the masses could be solved – within the framework of a one-party state – only by using extensive propaganda and mass-mobilization techniques. Indeed, the adoption of a Liberman-type reform in this situation could have aggravated the situation by, *inter alia,* leading to increased income differentials between enterprise managers and workers. Finally, and perhaps most important of all, Albania is the smallest country in Eastern Europe, both in size and population; in 1965 it had fewer than 2 million inhabitants. (The population in 1974 was approximately 2.4 million, mostly ethnic Albanians.) It was also geographically and politically isolated from its neighbouring countries, and led by a Party of Labour most carefully purged of all internal dissension. There was, therefore, no country in Eastern Europe in which circumstances were as favourable for the politicization of the entire population.

THE IDEOLOGICAL CAMPAIGNS

Before considering the results of the changes in the rules of the economic system, the ideological campaigns superimposed on the new planning system and designed to affect the desired politicization deserve some attention.

In February 1966 the Central Committee of the PLA issued a statement noting that, in response to the *Appeal*, many cadres had volunteered to work in production and it soon appeared that the *Appeal* had initiated a process of social metamorphosis whose high point was yet to come. On 4 March 1966 the Central Committee issued an 'Open Letter' to the population, the immediate consequences of which included a reduction by 15,000 in the number of state administrative employees (which the Albanian leadership may well have thought was made possible by the recent changes in economic planning), the abolition of military ranks and the introduction of political commissars into military units, the dispatching to the countryside of several intellectuals, managers, and party officials, and the replacement of an unspecific number of cadres in executive positions. There was also a narrowing of wage differentials, highly paid Albanians suffering a reduction in salaries. This last measure has since been used on several occasions, most recently on 1 April 1976, and its implications are considered in Chapter 6.

The speed and the extent of the changes that took place in Albania following the 'Open Letter' has been recorded in the official *History of the PLA:*

Within a record time the reorganizations of the state and party apparatus in the centre and in the districts on a sounder revolutionary basis was effected. The administrations of state enterprises and agricultural cooperatives were also reorganized and simplified. The number of ministries was reduced, unnecessary offices and branches were amalgamated. . . . The staff of the central state administration was reduced by half. About 15,000 cadres of the administration went over to production, especially in the countryside. A good number of cadres, among them top cadres of the Party and the state, were sent from the centre to the base. The simplification of the administrative apparatus was accompanied by a profound reduction of correspondence, thus replacing red tape with living work with the people. Reductions and simplifications were made also in the system of accounting and planning. Numerous tasks in the fields of planning and fixing prices, concentrated in the Council of Ministers, were passed over to the ministries and the executive committees of the district people's councils, always in line with the principle of democratic centralism.[17]

In addition to the increase in the labour force at the base provided by the 15,000 administrative employees, a campaign began to involve all state employees in physical production work. According to the *History,*

a major movement began, to link mental work with physical work with production. People engaged in mental work voluntarily went 'en masse' to help the peasantry in agricultural tasks. In line with the decision of the Central Committee to reorganize on a sounder basis the direct participation in production of men engaged in mental work, all the employees of the administration, men and women engaged in scientific and cultural work, started to work in production, particularly in the countryside, one month every year; in addition, tens of thousands of young people from high and middle schools participated in voluntary mass actions of construction and production.[18]

The Albanian leadership's interest in involving all members of society in physical work was not without precedent. In November 1958 the Central Committee of the PLA had resolved to involve all state employees and members of the government, including Central Committee members, in physical work. According to the resolution, all would spend one month a year in industry, agriculture, construction, or communal works. They would continue to receive their normal wage provided that they met a target set 30 per cent below that faced by a worker normally carrying out the particular task.

Several reasons for the introduction of these measures were put forward at the time. First, it was argued that voluntary participation in construction projects, particularly by the Albanian youth, had by now become a tradition. Second, it was necessary to increase the socialist consciousness of the population by convincing those normally otherwise employed that physical labour was the most important element in socialist construction. Experience of physical labour would also aid the fight against 'bureaucracy and petty-bourgeois tendencies', and would improve relations between workers and state functionaries.

The extent to which these measures were implemented in 1958 is unclear. The *PLA History* makes no mention of them, and even if for a time state officials were working in production as required, they were certainly no longer doing so in 1965. However, as already mentioned, the *Appeal* appears to have persuaded some of those engaged in 'mental' work to leave their desks for the work-bench, and the crucial implication of the subsequent 'Open Letter' was an increased emphasis on the politicization of life – in Chinese terminology, 'redness' was now to be placed above 'expertness'. It is clear that attempts had been made to bring workers closer to the process of plan determination, though the Albanian worker was still subject to a Labour Code that, though recently modified, contained penal sanctions and did little to encourage a sense of participation in the running of the economy. In September 1966, however, the changes that were apparently sweeping Albanian society found their way to the worker when the new Labour Code was issued.

It is perhaps useful to quote several of this new Code's articles:[19]

Article 3

In directing the economy of our country, our socialist state relies on the conscious participation of the workers and employees, and it supports the development of initiative and creative thinking in the working masses.

Article 6

The workers and employees have the right to organize in trade unions.

The trade unions of Albania are social organizations of the masses. They unite the workers and employees on a voluntary basis, and operate as a school of communist education under the leadership of the Party of Labour of Albania in accordance with its statutes.

Article 7

Organized into trade unions and conscious of the working-class mission to build socialism, the workers and employees participate in directing the economy, in drafting and realizing the state plans for economic development, in solving the problems of work and production, and in cultural activities and the increased well-being of the people.

The workers, employees, and their trade union organizations fight to strengthen discipline in the state and at work to continuously increase production, and to preserve and maintain state property. They control the administrative activity of enterprises, institutions, and organizations with the result that these groups function better, the people's government becomes stronger, and bureaucratic excesses may be avoided.

Article 9

The state organs take the position of the trade unions in the interpretation of the laws that regulate more important problems directly connected with work such as working conditions, wages, and social insurance for workers and employees.

Article 36

For work carried out outside normal work times, workers shall, in every case, be compensated only to the extent of 25 per cent above normal pay as fixed by the table of categories.

Article 48

The highest state organs and state inspection officers of the Health and Safety Division execute the provisions of this Code and its ordinances, resolutions and instructions dealing with problems of working conditions, working hours, vacation time, and safety and health measures. The rights and duties of the State Health and Safety Division are determined by decision of the Council of Ministers.

Whereas the old Labour Code had 264 articles, the new one has only 63. All reference to penal sanctions against workers is gone, and the new Code has a decidedly revolutionary tone. It should be noted that the role of the trade unions has changed dramatically compared with the role they played in 1959. Although Article 9 allows them a significant consultative role, it is clear from Article 48 that any decision-making power over working conditions that they may have had in the past has been transferred to the state hierarchy. The mobilization and education of workers is now seen as the major task of the trade unions, and the stipulations of Article 7 allowed the establishment of worker's control commissions in enterprises. Article 36 is significant in that it attempts to discourage overtime work as a means of increasing income: rather, the trend has been towards 'voluntary' overtime work, and there are many cases reported in the Albanian press of workers who, after finishing their jobs for the day, help in the construction of flats, schools, etc. Here, as in the case of the planning discussions, the distinctions between coercion and persuasion, and desired and actual implementation, are difficult to make.

Although the Fifth Congress of the PLA took place in November 1966, only a month after the appearance of the new Code, no mention was made of it by either Enver Hoxha or Mehmet Shehu in their respective speeches. There was, however, continued reference to workers' participation in planning, the revolutionization of life, and the ongoing fight against bureaucracy.

In a speech made on 6 February 1967,[20] Enver Hoxha stressed that, in solving problems of organization which arise in the state enterprise,

> the only correct and complete judgement is the check-up of the collective which verifies and should verify the case. This means 'the control by the masses' and 'the policy of the masses', all without exception, should submit to the judgement of the masses on their work and conduct in society. Communists should submit to a twofold control, to that of the Party and to that of the masses.

When new directors or other senior or technical staff were appointed to an enterprise, Hoxha argued, the new man should go before the workers' collective and give 'a frank account of himself so that the masses may pass judgement on him'. Further, the new employee or director should be told that if he blunders 'we will pull your ears', whereas if he keeps making mistakes, 'We will throw you overboard and bear well in mind that there is no one who can help you; the Party is ours, the regime is ours, it is we who are in power, it is the dictatorship of the proletariat which reigns. . . .' With respect to displays of bureaucratism, the solution rests again with the workers: 'the labouring masses should by all means and without hesitation strike down the director of this type or any other functionary of this kind, whoever and of whatever rank he may be in the Party or the government'.

One mechanism whereby this workers' control would take place would be in the wall newspaper. Albania, along with all the other socialist economies of Eastern Europe, had always used wall posters in their state enterprises, but Hoxha gave his opinion of these and was explicit about the need for changes:

> do away with the existing and very ridiculous wall newspapers and turn them into revolutionary wall bulletins which will help revolutionary education. Do away with these wall bulletins with their editorial boards of opportunist scribblers who uphold the dignity and authority of the director and of themselves at the same time, and let everyone

write what he thinks of work and of the people in bold face letters and without fear.

Hoxha also stressed the need for improving the circulation of cadres through the economy; all administrative and office workers should spend no less than 100 days of every year in production work – the period was shortly afterwards reduced to one month – and directors of enterprises should be changed regularly to prevent their 'bureaucratic stagnation'.

The implications of Hoxha's speech for worker's control were apparently significant. In several enterprises workers were reported to have been instrumental in solving problems of plan realization where state administration had failed. Examples quoted in *Zëri i popullit*, 5 July 1967, include the state Industrial Enterprise in Vlorë; where the use of lumber exceeding set norms was 'creating a serious problem, the manager of the enterprise asked some leading cadres to solve this problem with no results. The problem was then taken over by the collective, and the workers succeeded not only in stopping the excess use of lumber but even reduced its use by 30 per cent.' In the Shkodër State Construction Enterprise, when the plan for the first quarter of 1967 had not been met,

on their own initiative the workers asked the enterprise managers the reason for this setback. The answer they received didn't satisfy them, and they decided with good reason to exercise control over the administration of the enterprise. In a meeting which was held to find out results of the control, many deficiencies and shortcomings came to light in regard to the organization of the work for the implementation of the planned tasks. The workers then took the necessary measures and the situation then began to improve.

In addition to these spontaneous displays of workers' control, Hoxha's speech also allegedly gave rise to:

initiatives for the establishment of a revolutionary workers' control by organizing various control groups to deal with all the economic problems related to the successful implementation of the plans, and the regulation of all work in enterprises. Some of these are control groups to check the quality of products, the maintenance, and exploitation of machinery and the material inventory of the enterprise.

The trade unions were responsible for the organization of elections to the commissions, ensuring that candidate workers were ideologically and politically motivated. However, once elected, the commission was to be free to examine all aspects of the functioning of its enterprise, though its powers were advisory. Any significant problem it encountered was to be communicated to the entire collective of the enterprise, and management was expected to find a solution. The trade unions and party organs within the enterprise would doubtless be instrumental in applying pressure on the enterprise administration to ensure the effectiveness of the workers' control.

The foregoing discussion raises some questions but also permits some conclusions. It is, inevitably, difficult to gauge how far Hoxha was serious when he asked workers to criticize freely. However, even if he should be taken literally, the existing superior–subordinate relationships which had until then been officially endorsed could not be expected to change rapidly. Second, if the reports of improvements in efficiency resulting from acts of workers' control are true – and there is no reason to doubt them – it is clear that the organization of inputs to the production process in Albanian enterprises was far from optimal; and they also indicate that the changes made in the planning system in 1966 were not yet contributing significantly to enterprise efficiency. Third, it can be seen that the functions of the workers' control commissions were twofold. In the first place, the commissions were organs of control, intended to ensure that both the administrators and worker–collectives of the enterprises worked towards consistently fulfilling plans; their second function – integrally linked with the first – was to motivate fellow-workers.

It is clear that the movement for workers' control in Albania may be viewed as a logical extension of the attempts to involve the workers in planning. The distinction between these two increments of 'participation' is that, whereas the discussion of plans was intended for all workers, control functions were limited to the elected commissions. That these commissions were finding difficulties in their work became evident at the beginning of 1968. An article in *Bashkimi* noted that, over a nine-week period in 1967, egg breakages had not been entered as a loss in the accounts of the Mat district cooperatives; and the workers' control commission was criticized for failing properly to safeguard communist property. However, the most common and not unexpected problem faced by the commissions appeared to be interference from administrators:

> the efforts of some bureaucratic administrators to channel the control of workers' commissions into a bureaucratic framework according to 'Rules and Regulations' only shows their fear of the masses' revolutionary momentum. There is no other way to explain the tendency of some administrators to 'institutionalize' and to keep the workers' control under 'control'.[21]

The situation at the Pogradec handicraft cooperative is cited as a typical example. The chief accountant of this enterprise not only determined when the commission would meet, but also issued an eleven-page document entitled 'Regulations Concerning the Duties of Workers' Control', signed by himself and the enterprise director.

Shortly after this revelation of bureaucratic hindrance, the nature of workers' control in Albania was changed, taking on the form it has retained until the present time. The change arose as a consequence of a speech made by Enver Hoxha on 19 April 1968, entitled 'Working-class Control'. In it, Hoxha criticized the workers' control commissions as having yielded no positive results; 'not only this, they have become bureaucratic elements, they have eliminated the grass roots control, they have replaced the trade union committees, people from the administration have entered them as heads of the commissions', and this led to 'marked manifestations of revenge towards the workers' criticisms'. Consequently, Hoxha argued, while commissions composed entirely of workers might provide some measure of improvement, it would be best if the commissions were replaced entirely by 'direct workers' control'. Thus, workers' control committees would henceforth be elected on an *ad hoc* basis as particular problems arose, and their membership would be limited to workers engaged directly in production.

The change in the nature of workers' control in Albania may also be explained in terms of the hypothesis formulated earlier; namely, that if this type of control was primarily intended to put pressure on the enterprise director during the period of plan implementation – the plan having been drafted with the assistance of the worker participation mechanism – allowing representatives of management to sit on the commissions would possibly dilute their impact. The above-cited attempts by management to 'control' the commissions lend weight to this conjecture. Hoxha's proposal that control groups should be elected only when necessary might be expected to increase the flexibility of local party organs while limiting the possibility of undesired liaison between a permanent commission and management. However, the ultimate success or failure of workers' control would rest on the extent to which workers were in fact motivated to exert pressure on management. The PLA's attempts to bring worker's preferences into line with its own are discussed in the next chapter and Chapter 6.

It has already been noted that a scheme for workers' control was not to become the only manifestation of the dictatorship of the proletariat in Albania. On 28 April 1967, the Politbureau of the PLA issued a series of guidelines to the party apparatus on the circulation of cadres. The Politbureau suggested that the following criteria be used in determining the mechanism of job rotation.

(1) All state employees who have never experienced life at the

shop floor – in other words, who entered the central administration straight from school – should be dispatched to primary economic units immediately. In future no one who had spent less than five years at the base after leaving school should be admitted to the central administration.

(2) All cadres who had spent ten years in the central administration should also be sent off henceforth.

(3) As a rule, cadres should spend a minimum of three years at the base before they can return to the centre.

(4) An attempt should be made to substitute those who had long worked in senior positions in Tirana by staff from the provinces.

(5) In determining the destination for a cadre his educational and work experience should be taken into account.

(6) The circulation of cadres should apply within the various districts of the country as well as between the centre and the base, particular attention being paid to those local officials who display signs of bureaucratism.

(7) The management and technical staff of state enterprises and agricultural cooperatives need normally not be circulated because they are daily in close contact with the working masses.

(8) As many young people and women as possible should be employed in the central government and party offices.

(9) Emphasis should be placed on providing collective farms with experienced cadres and sending as many party members as possible to the production front in order to maintain a balanced distribution of communists and experts with the society.

(10) Direct participation in the production process should be used as a most effective means of educating cadres who make mistakes; however, this does not mean that reliable cadres should not be given difficult jobs.

(11) All institutions should draw up a plan for the circulation of cadres and submit it to their party committees to assist in the coordination of the scheme.[22]

Only one day later, the Central Committee of the PLA and the Council of Ministers issued a joint statement to the effect that, as a consequence of an allegedly spontaneous mass movement, 'the employees of ministries and central institutions, of party committees, executive committees, organizations of the masses, military cadres, teachers, and all intellectuals should spend 30 days a year directly in production, mainly in the countryside and in an organized way.[23] The one exception to this rule was to be that married women need spend only fifteen days a year in this way.

This renewed campaign for cadre participation in physical production was expected by the PLA to increase the level of proletarian consciousness of the cadres, thereby enhancing the dictatorship of the proletariat. In practical terms, however, the above scheme and the cadre circulation programme may be seen as an attempt by the PLA to increase its popularity with the workers at the expense of the cadres. The partial acceptance by the cadres of their new ideologically heightened (but materially reduced) situation in society was probably guaranteed by their peculiar vulnerability. In other words, the cadre whose personal ideology was in complete conflict with the PLA's could resist thirty days of production work or transfer to a cadre position elsewhere in the country only at the risk of being made a full-time proletarian, as indicated by point (10) of the guidelines of 27 April 1967.

The area in which these new revolutionary measures were likely to be most deeply felt was the central planning system. The exclusion of managers and other enterprise cadres from the circulation scheme (point (7) of the guidelines) represents a step backward from Hoxha's February 1967 position and indicates the PLA's desire to maintain stable conditions within the primary economic units – the farms and state enterprises. This is also suggested by the requirement that 'circulation' be planned (point 11); and the suggestion that a cadre's qualifications be taken into account in determining his new job (point 5) further indicates that the PLA felt economic necessity to be a constraint on its progress towards its ideological objectives. However, there is considerable evidence to suggest that the PLA's ideological campaign was not entirely successful, either politically or economically.

THE UNEXPECTED RESULTS: ORGANIZATIONAL

By June 1967 it was emerging through the Albanian press that the campaign for participation in physical production work was meeting opposition. One article discloses that even certain individuals who had been criticized in the press had not yet gone to the base. The regional party committees and executive committees of the people's councils are blamed for not ensuring the success of the schemes, and a determination to enforce participation is expressed. 'It is quite clear that these cadres who are avoiding production work possess a non-revolutionary bureaucratic mentality which must be fought mercilessly.' In *Zëri i popullit* of 24 March 1968 the internal situation is related to the changes taking place elsewhere in Eastern Europe, the 'revisionism' abroad being blamed on three factors: 'bureaucratism, intellectualism and technocratism'. The prescription for avoiding these evils is given as follows:

the long period of probation in state functions, the great unevenness of wages (a dangerous evil, this), and the privileges which they allegedly get as cadres (another dangerous evil) spoil them and incite them progressively to adopt, willy-nilly, features that are foreign to the proletarian class. Such phenomenon may also occur with cadres of worker origin and conditions, but this danger is greater to those coming from the peasantry and the intelligentsia. The cadres should be educated so as to realize that, even when they are working correctly, their departure from responsible functions and their going to work in the fold of the working class and the labouring masses is a necessity. It is to the advantage of the Party, for the present and the future.[24]

There is also evidence that the PLA's policy of replacing male functionaries by women, through the cadre circulation scheme (point (8) of the guidelines) was causing problems. The first party secretary of the Gjirokastër district suggested in an authorative journal that one of the ways in which resistance to the measures was manifesting itself was in attempts to discredit the new role of women:

[Some comrades] pursue a twofold aim; first, by creating difficulties for women they want to say, 'you see, we were right, women are incapable of directing'. Second, some of them, approaching the problem from a narrow, selfish point of view, act this way hoping that they can regain their 'lost position'.[25]

The PLA intensified the cadre circulation scheme following Enver Hoxha's speech on working-class control on 9 April 1968 by including enterprise directors and other cadres in primary economic units in it, and the aim of the scheme had by now been stated publicly as the elimination of bureaucracy in the state administration to preclude the onset of the revisionism which had destroyed socialism in the USSR. Thus, for example, it was alleged that 'cadres that have had long tenure but are professionally inept have acted in a conservative and egotistic manner by refusing to make room for new and capable revolutionary cadres'.[26] Likewise, 'great difficulties and obstacles have been encountered because of strong bureaucratic measures'.[27] On the relationship between workers' control and the administration, a party official stated:

The question of control by the working class (always under the guidance of the party and its teachings), including the question of raising the ideological level and improving administration work so as effectively to open the way to this control by purging the bureaucratic obstacles, must be the preoccupation of the party organization, a preoccupation that should be continual, systematic, and not merely for a day or a month.[28]

The problem of the dictatorship of the proletariat and its progress in Albanian society was the major topic for discussion at the Sixth Plenum of the Central Committee of the PLA, which assembled on 27 September 1968; and the Politbureau report to the Plenum provides evidence that the leadership was not satisfied with the results of the ideological campaign. In the report Ramiz Alia clarified the ideological motivation for the measures that had been carried out and pointed out areas in which the 'revolutionization' of society was encountering problems. With respect to ideology, Alia noted that:

Socialist revolution is uninterrupted evolution. It does not end either with the seizure of the reins of state or with the building of the economic base of socialism. The whole process of socialist and communist construction is the process of developing and deepening proletarian revolution in the political, economic, and ideological fields. Interrupting the revolutionary struggle, stopping the revolution half-way, is fatal to the destiny of socialism. The fact is that the class struggle, the struggle between the socialist and capitalist ways, continues throughout the period of transition from capitalism to communism. This is the fundamental contradiction all through this period.[29]

The report, on behalf of the Party leadership, was of key importance at the time in dividing into four groups the socioeconomic issues over which the PLA sought influence. The neologisms that identified the negative features of each relationship were characteristic of the contemporary presentation of topics for party or public information, but were none the less valid expressions of the new policy foreshadowed by the report.

The first issue was termed 'bureaucracy':

Failure to set and continuously perfect these relations along correct socialist lines will inevitably lead to the emergence of bureaucratism and to the degeneration of cadres who, from being servants of the people, gradually turn to a new bourgeois class which follows a bourgeois policy and uses its power to secure a privileged position for itself and to hold sway over the people. This sets up relations of oppression and exploitation between this stratum and the masses. Social ownership gradually loses its socialist nature and turns into ownership of the state capitalist type.

The frequent transfer of managers, technicians, and officials between posts with intermissions for physical labour was seen as the appropriate mitigation, but the report indicated that the schemes already started on these lines had encountered resistance.

The second group of issues included 'technocratism', 'economism', and 'intellectualism', united by the common trait of arrogance in professional judgements. The report argued that priority should be given to ideological over technical education. The basis for concern over intellectuals was similar to, though not identical with, that for cadres. The problem arose

not because of their nature; but, because of their tendency to detach mental from physical labour, their position and the role they play in leading and organizing work, and the individual nature of their work, the intellectuals are susceptible to alien bourgeois and revisionist viewpoints, ideology, politics, and ethics; they are inclined to detach themselves from the masses, to overrate their role, ability, and talents, to place themselves above the masses, to slip into postures of egotism, intellectualism, and self-conceit, to consider themselves the only force capable of directing and leading. Therefore it is here that a very important area of the class struggle lies.

'Conservatism' was perceived as the third problem, to be countered by implementing measures for the increased mechanization of production processes in the Albanian economy which had been outlined by the Third Plenum of the Central Committee of the PLA (13–14 October 1967). The report accused managers of conservatism in refusing to implement labour-saving changes in technology (technical progress in Albania is here discussed in Chapters 3 and 5); and it also argued that in the political sphere conservatism had led to opposition to the appointment of young cadres in various positions throughout the society. It posed the rhetorical question:

If we fail to train and promote new cadres right away, then when shall we do it? Our comrades must never forget that when our Party and People trusted them for the first time with posts of great responsibility, they were not only very young in years but did not have that culture and those skills that the new cadres, carefully educated by the Party and marked with its ideology and a wide range of professional skills, boast of today. . . . The struggle against conservatism is a long and perpetual one. It will never end because our society keeps developing; some things always spring up and grow while others become obsolete and should be discarded.

Finally, though no term was coined, the report spoke of the conflict between personal and social interest. It is noted that this tendency

is manifested not only in the material sphere, in the running after money and a fat salary, after privileges and material advantages, in the tendency to contribute as little as possible and wrest as much as possible from society in occupying a comfortable post in town. It is manifested in a thousand and one more forms, extending also to the moral features involving one's own character like egotism and individualism, envy and personal ambition, intrigues and lies, career-seeking and servility, arrogance and self-conceit, comfort and ease, personal glory and familiarity, nepotism, acquiescence, and apathy, localism and partiality, and so on and so forth. This means that there are many problems; there is a whole field of action to imbue the people with the norms of communist ethics and to educate them to place the revolution above everything else.

Measures to enhance social motivation should not, the report stressed, go to the point at which real personal incomes of workers and peasants did not steadily increase or inequalities between them and cadres (and between farmers in different areas and on different types of farms) diminish. (This question is taken up in greater detail in Chapter 5.)

The following analysis of the economic problems arising from the 1965 and 1966 changes in the rules of the system will attempt to show that, from a purely economic point of view, the decentralization measures of 1966, however moderate, militated against increased efficiency. On the other hand, the PLA's goals of greater control and maintenance of power in Albania evidently required a decentralization of economic decision-making power.

THE UNEXPECTED RESULTS: ECONOMIC

It is perhaps surprising, given the PLA's emphasis on ideological campaigns and central planning, that there should be accounts in the Albanian press in 1967 complaining of widespread private, and thus illegal, economic activity. Durrës workers are criticized for failing to denounce 'the embezzlers and misusers of socialist property'. Another article argues that base-level party organizations should intensify the class struggle against workers who behave 'as if they were landowners, artisans, and workers in private service, middlemen in the distribution sphere, entrepreneurs for other work, etc.'. It points out that in Pogradeç, Elbasan, and Shkodër, among other places, many people were realizing large incomes from orchards in which they were employing others, and were also holding stock until the price was at its highest before selling. The article also indicates that there were a number of private handicraftsmen, acting as clothes-dealers, tailors, carpenters etc., without a trade licence. Even worse, it is stated that many people employed by the state spent their day at work 'resting' so they could slave at night to earn income illegally. By 1959 most artisans had been brought into cooperatives, but this apparently did not prevent them from cheating and failing to declare income. Finally, it is disclosed that there were private entrepreneurs carrying out repairs and construction work at factory sites, houses, and schools. The example is given of two such entrepreneurs who were engaged by a collective farm in Lushnjë to build a palace of culture for 800,000 leks (the official exchange rate at that time was 50 leks to 1 dollar). These private builders were allegedly obtaining their resources through bribery and corruption, and were being commissioned by directors of state or collective organizations who were behind in meeting their plans. The article concluded that the problems were not economic but ideological, that bourgeois thoughts from the past were the cause, and that if worker persuasion could not solve the problem, harsher punishment would have to be used.

If such problems existed in March 1967, it is clear that the PLA's ideological campaign, which had begun with the initiation of workers' involvement in planning in the middle of 1965, was not having the desired impact. Such problems – familiar in all Soviet-type economies – as the poor quality and shortages of consumer goods and the failure of enterprises to fulfil assortment plans, while overfulfilling the plan for global output, were also reported. Discontent was expressed with the quality of packaging and content of export goods. In the transport sector, it was disclosed that state-owned trucks and cars were being used for picnics and excursions and for the transport of workers' relatives to various 'unplanned' destinations, and also that trucks had been discovered travelling on planned routes without any cargo, the drivers apparently being unaware of the situation. The existence of more unusual dysfunctions was revealed in an analysis of the Albanian statistical system which may be summarized as follows.

In 1966 two changes had been made in the Albanian statistical system. First, it was decided that 80 per cent of the statistics submitted by the enterprises to the central authorities were unnecessary and their collection was consequently eliminated. Second, in order to save the time of experts in the Executive Committees of the People's Councils, the ministries and the Directorate of Statistics, it was decided that statistics would henceforth be sent to only one department in each organ. A surprisingly large number of problems had arisen in connection with this apparently simple reorganization. The economist Jakubini argues that insufficient care had been taken to explain to all concerned that, along with the reductions in statistical reporting, it was 'necessary to eradicate and condemn the erroneous concepts of those who overrate records'. There had been certain instances of actual increases in data collection and cases of people asking for statistics when, according to the guidelines of the Directorate of Statistics, they did not have the right to do so and were thus breaking the law. Whereas it was stipulated that enterprises should prepare output statistics for collection by Executive Committees and ministries every three months, some higher organs were demanding that they be submitted monthly. Jakubini points out that, in addition to being illegal, this practice also reflected an undesirable stress on 'globalism' when concentration on the quantity and quality of individual goods was necessary. There was also evidence of globalism in the construction and transport sectors, although here it was merely undesirable, not illegal. Finally, it was indicated that statistics were often being submitted late and sometimes were even sent to the wrong place.

However, it seems that ignorance of the rules was in evidence throughout the planning and management system. An article in the July–August 1968 issue of *Ekonomia popullore* noted that contracts between enterprises were often not drawn up because the buyer did not know where to send his order. Thus, it might be sent to an Executive Committee when a ministry was responsible for the distribution of the relevant product. The article went on to note that *rreth* Executive Committees often praised enterprises for fulfilling global output plans when assortment was under-fulfilled. Finally, it was indicated that in several districts the Executive Committee would ensure the production of goods necessary as inputs elsewhere in its own district while ignoring the requirements of the rest of the economy.

All of these dysfunctions were blamed on a lack of knowledge or understanding of the rules; but given the pressure of the ideological campaigns and the scarcity of properly qualified state functionaries at the local level, it is hardly surprising that such problems occurred.

However, the *de facto* decentralization of investment decisions was, from an ideological viewpoint, by far the most critical unexpected outcome of the changes, since it implied an increased role for the law of value in the state sector of the economy. As part of the 1966 changes in economic planning and management, it had been decided to place enterprise funds for investment and construction under the jurisdiction of the ministries and the Executive Committees of the People's Councils. These bodies would then be able to determine the precise distribution of funds among alternative projects without the projects being subject to state bank control. In making this decision, the PLA leadership was evidently unaware of the importance of bank control in the classic Soviet model, in that – theoretically at least – it provides a check on how subordinate financial units in the hierarchy are carrying out the duties assigned to them. But however important it may be to have a check on the activity of ministries and Executive Committees in a centralized economy, it is still more important to have such a check in a decentralized system. In other words, if there is a decentralization of economic decision-making power within the policy, planning, and administrative hierarchy – as there was in Albania in 1966 – and the authorities do not want this decentralization to spread down to the primary economic units, then a check on the activity of the regional authorities is necessary.

While it might be argued that in an essentially non-market, administered system the regional authorities would normally have no incentive to relax their control over enterprise directors, the Albanian case is complicated by the ideological campaigns. If a member of a People's Council Executive Committee is expected to be ideologically pure, it might be in his best interests to spend his time organizing revolutionary meetings of workers, and to allow the enterprise director under his jurisdiction – who probably knows more about the economics of the situation anyway – to determine how best to allocate investment funds. From the director's point of view this newly gained power will help him fulfil his plans and thus gain the attendant bonuses. According to official estimates, decentralized – illegal – investment accounted for rather more than 1 per cent of total investment in the Albanian economy in 1968, which may have been no more than the tip of the iceberg. If so, it can be argued that the ideological campaigns led directly to the most undesired dysfunction in a socialist economy – the weakening of the state plan. Articles in the Albanian press in 1968 complained of enterprises embarking on illegal construction projects before the end of the plan period and, being unable to complete them, presenting the planners with a *fait accompli* for the allocation of funds to complete the projects in the next plan period – again a familiar complaint in the USSR and throughout Eastern Europe.

The official reaction to decentralized investment was understandably violent, although precise details of punishment for offenders have not been published. However, it is clear that the authorities did not associate the problem with the ideological campaigns in the manner argued above. Rather, it was assumed that vestiges of the past and other alien ideologies were to blame, the implication being that the campaigns had not yielded the desired degree of political education of the majority of cadres. There has since been no further mention of decentralized investment in the Albanian press, and the fact that the leadership felt confident in 1970 to embark on a further decentralization – discussed below – suggests that the problem was somehow solved, probably through the reimposition of bank control.

It has already been suggested that the decentralization measures of 1966 may have militated against more efficient resource allocation in the Albanian economy. Since the decentralization of economic decision-making power in a centrally administered system generally tends to improve information flows and make possible increased use of commodity-money (market) relations, thus improving efficiency, the contention that in Albania the outcome might have been different requires explanation. It was noted earlier that the Soviet system of plan indicators was not fully adopted in Albania until 1959, fourteen years after the PLA's ascent to power. This delay was caused partly by the authorities' unwillingness, for political reasons, to centralize the economic system, and partly because there were too few trained economists to man such a system. Similarly, it is doubtful whether the number of qualified cadres necessary for effective decentralization was present in 1965. This point may be clarified by reference to the difference between the pre-1959 decentralized system and the later, post-1966, system. Thus, prior to the establishment of the classic Soviet model, some allocative decisions were taken by enterprises; and, to the extent that managements' goals differed from those of the PLA leadership, the outcomes would be different from those intended by the party. The post-1966 rules required that local party and state functionaries, and not managers, took economic decisions; and the system was specifically designed to ensure the allocation of resources in accordance with a centrally ratified plan. But this required cadres who were politically and economically qualified, both at the centre and at the base. If the PLA leadership had been motivated purely by a desire for efficiency, they would have kept the country's experts concentrated at the centre until the education system had produced sufficient new cadres to spread throughout the economy. But they were not so motivated, and the new system rules had in any case been expected to lead to centrally desired outcomes more effectively than had the classical Soviet model. In fact, there is evidence that the new system was not completely meeting the objectives of increased party control at all levels and rapid economic growth rates. To be sure, as is indicated in a later chapter, the targets of the Fourth Five-year Plan were exceeded in most sectors, but this was probably due more to massive capital inflows from China than to the efficiency of the system.

The two areas in which the system rules might again be changed without difficulty and with the possibility of improved results were, first, the plan indicators and, second, the distribution of decision-making power between the ministries and the Executive Committees. A reduction in the number of indicators requiring hierarchical approval would ease the pressure on inexperienced cadres, while a limitation on the number of enterprises under ministerial control to those in priority sectors of production would possibly facilitate economic growth by removing the burden on the ministries of planning the non-priority sectors.

It should be noted that a reduction in the number of plan indicators does not necessarily imply increased scope for market relations in the state sector. A multiplicity of indicators referring to one allocation decision may result in contradictory instructions to management – for example, an enterprise's plans for labour and material inputs inconsistent with the plan for quantity of output. In such a situation it is at least possible that simplification may enhance central control over the priority objectives. On the other hand, the Albanian experience in 1968 showed that certain indicators could be removed from central determination and supervision only at great risk – in this case, financial control over investment decisions. That changes reflecting an awareness of these points were imminent was indicated when the Ninth Plenum of the PLA Central Committee – convened towards the end of 1969 – called for a thorough re-examination of the planning methodology with a view to improving its 'scientific content'.

THE 1970 REORGANIZATION OF THE PLANNING AND MANAGEMENT SYSTEM

The reorganization of the planning system was announced by Hysni Kapo in his report to the Tenth Plenum of the Central Committee of the PLA in June 1970. He gave the major aims of the changes as being to 'do away with routine and raise the work of management to a scientific basis' and further to improve worker participation in the system. On the first point, he did not provide much amplification, merely noting that as many workers and cadres as possible must become acquainted with the economic laws of socialism, thus confirming the existence of the cadre education problem suggested above. With respect to worker participation, he argued that the participation of the workers in planning was being stifled by excessive centralization of decision-making on economic issues which could best be resolved at the district level. Thus, while the reorganization of 1966 had proved helpful, it was now necessary to expand the competence of the base even further. Kapo also argued that proposals on the productive activity of the enterprise made by workers were not finding their way into the plans because of excessive red tape in the hierarchy. This problem could be overcome only if more enterprises were placed under the control of the Executive Committees of the local People's Councils and if the number of plan indicators facing the enterprise was reduced and their quality raised.

In terms of a redistribution of economic decision-making power, the 1970 reform appears to have been fairly far-reaching. In 1960 only 20 per cent of enterprises were under the jurisdiction of the Executive

Committees: this number had grown to 40 per cent in 1969 (accounting for 30 per cent of total industrial production) and 80 per cent in 1971.[30] The percentage share of these enterprises in total production is not known, but, given the small average size of firms, it was probably still not large.)

The initiation of each round of Five-year-Plan elaboration is vested in the party. Its guidelines pass from the State Planning Commission via either the ministries or the People's Councils to the enterprise. It is within the enterprise that the bulk of the detailed draft planning is carried out, and this process is considered in more detail below. Thereafter the individual plans of the primary economic units pass back to the State Planning Commission, again via the ministry or Executive Committee. It is the task of the State Planning Commission to amend the individual plans so that a single balanced plan for the economy is obtained. The plan then becomes law, and the enterprise receives its tasks for the coming five years. These plan targets are further disaggregated annually, the process of annual compilation being essentially the same.

At the enterprise level, the drawing up of annual plans begins in July of the pre-plan year. At plant and enterprise levels, commissions of planning are set up, composed mainly of workers. At the brigade level, work groups are established. These commissions and groups analyse the performance of the enterprise over the first six months of the base year with a view to determining possible levels of production for the remainder of the year. These data are then used by the planning commission, in conjunction with the enterprise director, to draw up a set of plan proposals to be put before the work collective. Throughout this process, the Five-year Plan should also be taken into account.

The next step in the process involves 'the organization of ideo-political and propagandistic work with workers for the drawing-up of the project plan'. The trade union and party organizations in the enterprise use wall posters and emulation notice boards to encourage workers to make proposals about ways in which the tasks of the firm may be carried out more successfully. These proposals are then all checked for their likely contributions to productivity, etc. On the basis of the original plan proposals of the commissions and work groups, and the proposals made by workers, the project plan is drawn up. This plan is then brought before a mass meeting of workers again and, when approved, is sent to the relevant higher authority within the state administration. Following the drafting of the national plan by the State Planning Commission, the plan for each enterprise finds its way back down the hierarchy. The final plan is now brought before the meeting of the worker collective and explained to it, particular attention being paid to a discussion of any changes that had to be made by the superior organs.

It must be re-emphasized that the foregoing scenario is designed specifically for the motivation of enterprise workers; the PLA hopes that it can thus mobilize the workers to press for higher plan targets than would normally be acceptable to management. Indeed, in contrast with the reforms that have taken place elsewhere in Eastern Europe, the position of the Albanian enterprise director has continually deteriorated. Materially, he has suffered several cut-backs of salary during the 1960s and 1970s; and in terms of power, his authority over the activity of his enterprise has been diminished by a change in the Albanian concept of one-man management. Whereas this term had previously been rendered in Albanian as *udhëheqjeunike*, a literal translation of the Russian *edinonachalie* (one-man management), this has now become *drejtim unik* (single guidance), the term always being appended with statements such as 'under the leadership of the enterprise party organization'. Finally, the use by the PLA of worker participation and workers' control schemes has meant that the director is now under pressure from both the state hierarchy above and the workers' organizations below. It has already been mentioned that by 1968 enterprise directors were benefiting from a *de facto* decentralization probably caused by the zeal of the ideological campaigns and the removal of bank control over investments. Now it appears that this gain has been removed, and that the director has lost most of the decision-making power he ever had. However, he remains responsible for the enterprise's achieving its plan targets once these are confirmed.

A phrase often encountered in the Albanian literature surrounding the present planning system is that it has increased markedly the 'initiative' of the primary economic units in the planning process. On the basis of such remarks, it might be supposed that there has been a decentralization of decision-making power to the enterprise in the manner of other East European reforms. However, as an examination of the table of plan indicators (Appendix Table A1) shows, the notion of increased initiative can really be applied meaningfully only to the worker participation schemes, specifically in their ideological aspects. The enterprise has the power to approve only plan 8(c), which deals with the measures to be taken for the exploitation of internal reserves, clearly an area of involvement for worker participation groups and the resident party organization.[31] The number of indicators in the plan can be seen from the table to be only 36. This appears to be a significant reduction, compared with the 77 indicators used before 1970, but it is difficult to imagine what the removed 41 indicators referred to, let alone to speculate about the nature of the original, pre-1966, 550 plan indicators.

At the macroeconomic level, the planning procedures remain as they were in 1959. Thus, the major method of plan formation remains the 'method of balances', and as late as August 1976 a well-known Albanian economist felt obliged to write that balances were still not being drawn up correctly and for all sectors of the economy. Ideological considerations preclude any discussion of optimal planning of the Albanian economy, mathematical techniques being used only at enterprise level, while at the centre attempts are being made to compile an input–output table. However, the table does not appear yet (1980) to have been completed, and it is noticeable that, after a period of apparent enthusiasm in 1971 and 1972, the number of articles on mathematical economics appearing in the Albanian literature diminished. This may be linked with the dismissal of certain economic ministers discussed below and in Chapter 3.

During the period of plan implementation, socialist emulation campaigns are used to elicit greater work effort. These campaigns range from competitions between members of a brigade at enterprise level to inter-enterprise and inter-district competitions, and winners receive prizes such as red flags (moral incentive) and free holidays (material incentive).

THE PROBLEMS OF THE CONTEMPORARY SYSTEM

The problems arising from the contemporary system may be classified into three groups: the persistence of 'globalism' in plan fulfillment; the existence of widespread absenteeism among the labour force and low work norms; and the re-emergence of small-scale private economic activity. Thus, whereas the global implementation of the first two years of the Fifth Five-year Plan (1971–5) was 'satisfactory', many individual sectors failed to meet their targets. In May 1973 the Ministry of Trade announced that, although many shops had been built in new towns, the selection of goods in them was poor, owing to failure on the part of enterprises to meet contractual obligations and to 'globalism'. Enterprises producing consumer goods were again blamed early in 1974 for failing to meet assortment and quality plans, it being argued that this problem could be solved only if the local party organizations raised the ideological level of workers. Perhaps the best example of the extent of this problem is provided by the report that, for the first nine months of 1972, plans for global industrial output in the districts of Korça and Elbasan were, respectively, 102.3 per cent and 102 per cent fulfilled, whereas the targets for output in physical units were met to the extent of some 49 and 62 per cent.[32]

Whereas the PLA has attempted to overcome this problem by

undertaking education campaigns with the workers, insufficient effort appears to have been made to improve output mix by offering material incentives. The law of 1967 on the special enterprise fund gives equal weighting to the fulfilment of production, cost-reduction, and profit plans in the distribution of managerial bonuses, and production plan fulfilment is determined 'according to . . . the evaluation made by the directing administrative organ'.[33] The ministries and Executive Committees have clearly not placed sufficient emphasis on assortment in their bonus determinations, though they appear to have had the power to do so, and the ideological campaigns have not yet borne fruit. It seems unlikely that material incentives will be used more effectively in the near future, because in April 1976 enterprise directors 're-nounced all forms of supplementary income.[34] (See Chapter 5 on the PLA's measures leading to this 'renunciation'.)

The widespread labour absenteeism in the Albanian economy has already been mentioned, and the 1970 changes in the system have had no apparent impact on the problem. It was reported that some workers in the Buqizë chrome mines averaged only twenty work days per month in 1972, and that industrial enterprises of the Skrapar district lost 14,456 working days through unjustified absenteeism. There is in fact evidence to support the contention that planning is, by and large, 'slack' in the Albanian economy rather than 'taut', if seen from the worker's point of view. Failure to receive supplies on time often leaves workers with nothing to do while still being paid, while work norms if they are imposed at all – are often easily fulfilled. But in 1973 only 10 per cent of the workforce were being given norms at all. As in the case of 'globalism', the PLA has blamed labour problems on insufficient revolutionary spirit among the population. However, any tendency to match employment plans to output targets rather than to availability of material inputs – themselves inadequate in relation to output targets – could also provide part of the explanation, together with a preference for 'keeping unemployment inside the factory gate' in a relatively labour-abundant economy.

The re-emergence of private business activity in the Albanian economy is, however, also an indication of the relative failure of the PLA's ideological campaigns. As recently as 1975, it was admitted that tailors, carpenters, builders, and cooperative farmers – some even party members – were engaged in private, profit-making ventures. The two most serious implications of this illegal activity were argued to be the theft of materials from state stocks and relaxation at legal work to save energy for private activities. In the context of cadre movements into the countryside to assist in agricultural work, one report pointed out that many collective farmers were drifting into towns to set up private businesses and become 'petty bourgeois'. In this, they were allegedly often being assisted by party members.

The ideological education of the workers is conducted by the local trade union organization under the direction of the enterprise party committee. In April 1977 all workers were being required to attend a weekly one-hour class, in which the documents of the November 1976 PLA Congress were studied and, although attendance at the classes was officially voluntary, the names of absent workers were prominently displayed on factory notice boards. Ideologically motivated social activities are also organized in enterprises by the women's and youth committees.

There is evidence to suggest that Albanian workers are becoming aware of the general economic implications of the PLA ideology that they have studied. Thus, workers in several Albanian enterprises visited by the author in 1977 indicated that, as a consequence of the Seventh Party Congress, they would work harder to improve the quality of products, prevent waste of raw materials, and even devote some of their spare time to agricultural work, particularly at harvest time. On the other hand, when asked questions specifically related to their particular work, most indicated that work was easy and that norms were either at appropriate or at low levels. The existence of slack output plans in much of the Albanian economy is also indicated by the extent to which they are often over-fulfilled. It is equally true that when a plan target is not met, the margin often appears to be rather large, but this may be due to delays in deliveries of capital equipment from China, or to the PLA's over-optimism in planning following an illusory success, or to inadequate co-ordination of available material inputs with output targets.

It seems reasonable to argue, however, that the role previously played by the enterprise director in obtaining slack plans has now been taken over by the workers. Thus, although poor workers are subjected to embarrassment by being pointed out at meetings and made to perform self-criticism, and this has probably led to a greater homogeneity of work effort within the enterprise, there is nothing in the rules of the system to ensure that the work level is not generally low, and the increasing use of group rather than individual, bonuses tied to plan fulfilment has probably reinforced this tendency.

It seems reasonable to conclude that the changes made to the Albanian planning system since 1965 have, in economic content, involved simplification and marginal adjustment rather than radical change. More generally, they have been designed to improve the PLA's control over the economy and to increase pressure on enterprise management through the worker 'control' and 'participation' mechanisms. To the extent that these latter innovations have contributed to the PLA's popularity in the country, its goal of staying in power has been met the more easily. On the other hand, rapid economic growth is unlikely to have been promoted more satisfactorily under the later rules and practices than was the case prior to 1965, largely because the PLA's assumption that pressure from below will yield greater efficiency and higher levels of output depends for its validity on an ideologically well educated and highly motivated workforce. Although the ideological campaigns conducted since 1965 have probably had some impact on the workings of the system – there has been a notable reduction in the number of complaints about 'hidden reserves' since 1970 – they can hardly be labelled as an unqualified success.

CONCLUSION

The development of the Albanian planning and management system up to the late 1970s has reflected the PLA's desire to establish a set of rules and practices that would maximize the leadership's influence over economic developments and prevent any political opponents from removing them from power. While there has been some decentralization, leakage of decision-making power from the ministries or People's Councils to the enterprise has been minimal, with the significant exception of some loss of central control over the investment pattern following the lifting of bank supervision. However, there is evidence to suggest that this decision has now been reversed; and, in his report to the Seventh PLA Congress in November 1976, Enver Hoxha indicated that the leadership was well aware of the importance of financial control: 'By strengthening their dynamic control by means of money, the financial and banking organs must become a barrier to any action which runs counter to the discipline of the plan and good financial order.'[35]

The PLA leadership's desire to maintain power was undoubtedly important in slowing the rate of centralization in the 1950s and, perhaps even more crucial, in leading to the institution of schemes for worker participation in the mid-1960s. To the extent that the latter measures increased PLA popularity with the workers, the changes in the system may have contributed towards the leadership's achievement of its goal. However, increased popularity for the leadership must be distinguished from heightened ideological commitment on the part of workers. In the latter sense, the ideological campaigns have probably failed as yet to yield the desired results. On the other hand, it is probably too early to dismiss the campaigns as having been doomed to failure from the outset.

Any conclusion about the effectiveness of the Albanian system of economic planning and management in encouraging a high rate of industrial growth must be postponed until the PLA's development strategy has been analysed in the chapters to follow. However, it is possible to make several preliminary observations on this issue. First, it may be argued that, if a government's development strategy requires that economic growth be very fast in some sectors of the economy at the expense of others, then some degree of central planning is necessary; and it is argued later that this has clearly been the case in Albania. Then it follows that the planning and management system will be important, not only in the obvious sense that it formulates the plans, but also in influencing the extent to which individual economic agents are prepared to work towards fulfilling those plans. Thus, the ideological campaigns and the worker participation and control schemes have been as much variables helping to determine the outcome of the leadership's development strategy as elements in the leadership's strategy for retaining power. The link between the PLA's development strategy and the motivational aspects of the rules of the system is considered in Chapter 5.

It has already been suggested that PLA ideology has been to follow strictly the guidelines of *Economic Problems of Socialism in the USSR*, and it may be concluded that, with the exception of the above-mentioned misunderstanding with respect to financial control, this has been consistently reflected by Albanian practice in developing the planning and management system. On the other hand, the ideological campaigns following the March 1966 'Open Letter' may have contributed to the leakage of economic decision-making power into the enterprise which became apparent by 1968. However, the apparent reversal of this tendency in 1970, without seemingly weakening the campaigns, suggests that the campaigns were not, *per se*, contrary to Stalinist requirements. Indeed, to the extent that PLA influence over the economy has been extended by the changes in the system since 1965, it may even be argued that the PLA leadership has devised a set of system rules more Stalinist than those of the classical Soviet model. Indeed, it might also be argued that the apparent withdrawal of the 'redness' factor in the location of Chinese planning decisions in the middle of 1977, while it remains a priority in Albania, has contributed towards the deterioration of relations between Tirana and Peking.

At no stage has the notion that economic decision-making should be decentralized to the enterprise – in the manner of other East European reforms – been entertained in public, although Enver Hoxha, in his report to the Seventh Congress of the PLA in November 1976, accused former State Planning Commission Chairman Abdyl Këllezi of striving

in every way to distort the principles of our socialist planning, in order to divest it of its socialist content and to set our economy on the road to revisionist self-management. This hostile, anti-Marxist activity was severely and strongly dealt with by the party and prevented from finding any field in which it could operate.[36]

The discussion of Albanian industrial development during the Fifth Five-year Plan – in the next chapter – suggests that the dismissal of Këllezi and others was probably due more to disagreement over the content of the plans than to conflict about the loci of economic decision-making. However, if a suggestion to decentralize economic decision-making really was a major factor in the purging of Këllezi, then it can be concluded that the Albanian economic system will not see any reforms of the type initiated elsewhere in Eastern Europe while Enver Hoxha remains First Secretary of the PLA.

CHAPTER 3

ALBANIAN INDUSTRIAL DEVELOPMENT, 1945–1977

The establishment of a set of system rules that limits the extent of enterprise decision-making to attempts at mass mobilization should in principle enable the central planners to determine the pattern of economic development by allocating resources in accordance with their preferences. The nature of those allocation decisions, particularly within the industrial sector, is the subject of this chapter.

THE STALINIST DEVELOPMENT STRATEGY

The most succinct formulation of the Stalinist development strategy is to be found in Stalin's *Economic Problems of Socialism in the USSR*. Here, Stalin provides two important 'laws' to guide industrialization policy. The first of these, called the 'basic economic law of socialism', is formulated as 'the securing of the maximum satisfaction of the constantly rising material and cultural requirements of the whole of society through the continuous expansion and perfection of socialist production on the basis of higher techniques'.[1]

The second law forms part of Stalin's preconditions for the transition to communism:

> It is necessary . . . to ensure . . . a continuous expansion of all social production, with a relatively higher rate of expansion of the production of means of production. The relatively higher rate of expansion of production of the means of production is necessary not only because it has to provide the equipment both for its own plants and for all other branches of the economy, but also because reproduction on an extended scale becomes altogether impossible without it.[2]

For Albanian political economy, the 'basic economic law' represents both the goal of socialist production and the means for its attainment. The 'goal-means scheme . . . expresses the two parts in the dialectical unity of the basic economic law of socialism'.[3] It is argued that, the greater the volume of production at low cost and high quality and the higher the rate of growth of total output, the better will the needs of the population be satisfied. A precise definition of 'higher techniques' follows only from the discussion of the second major development law: 'The operation of the law of priority growth of production of the means of production springs directly from the need continually to perfect techniques and systematically to increase the productivity of social labour.'[4]

It is explained that the productivity of social labour will rise only as the proportion of living to embodied labour involved in the production of each unit of output falls. In other words, techniques are perfected by introducing labour-saving innovations; in the long term the capital–labour ratio must rise.

In the industrial sector, the 'priority law' requires the rate of growth of output of group A to be higher than that of group B. However, as Peter Wiles has noted, this does not correspond exactly with the notions of investment goods and consumption goods.[5] Thus, while group B is the set of all consumer goods produced by the industrial sector, group A output includes not only capital goods but also all intermediate production. Thus, if by 'reproduction on an extended scale' Stalin means an acceleration of growth, group A production 'must plainly increase faster than the rest simply because it must increase first'.[6] On the other hand, as Wiles has also pointed out, the priority law does not hold under all possible assumptions. However, the Albanians simply accept the law without question, adding one further possible misinterpretation: namely, that giving priority to group A implies priority for heavy industry – and this is almost certainly a borrowing from Stalinist practice. However, provided that a feasible development strategy is implied by the Albanian interpretation of Stalin's laws, it does not, perhaps, matter very much whether economic growth could be achieved in other ways or even whether Stalin misinterpreted his own laws.

One may apply several empirical tests to see whether the facts of Albania's economic development are consistent with the apparent requirements and goals of a Stalinist development strategy. First, it is necessary that the capital–labour ratio be rising. There have been no official estimates of the Albanian capital–labour ratio published; however, on the basis of available statistics it is possible to obtain a sufficiently reasonable estimate of the changing ratio for the industrial sector. In agriculture, with increasing levels of mechanization and a sharply falling population relative to other sectors, the ratio may reasonably be assumed to have risen over the past thirty years.

Table 3.1 gives estimates of the rise of labour productivity in industry. What changes in the capital–labour ratio can be reasonably supposed to underlie this rise in labour productivity? It has been argued that, 'in a fast-growing economy such as the Soviet Union, [current provisions for depreciation based on a straight-line principle] seriously over-estimate retirements, and gross investment is a far better approximation to new investment than is net investment'.[7] Thus, according to calculations made by Domar, in an economy with a constant rate of growth of 10 per cent per annum and a stock of capital which needs to be replaced every 30 years, if all machinery is replaced at the appointed time, 95 per cent of gross investment will be new investment – that is, will represent increases in capacity. In an economy with a rate of growth of 3 per cent per annum and the same average length of life of assets, only 63 per cent of gross investment will represent increases in capacity.[8]

TABLE 3.1 *Output and productivity in industry*

	1950	*1955*	*1960*	*1963*	*1970*	*1973*	*1975*
Global industrial product (million leks in 1971 prices)	461	1,275	2,781	3,385	7,104	9,608	10,798
Industrial labour force	16,337	28,964	48,074	66,941	106,223	121,602	133,437
Labour productivity (leks/man)	28,219	44,020	57,848	50,567	66,878	79,012	80,992

Source: see Appendix C.

Thus, in the Albanian case, where the rate of growth of industrial output has averaged well over 10 per cent per annum since 1950, it seems reasonable to measure increases in the capital stock by gross investment. Further, assuming that half of all investment between 1945 and 1950 was in industry, and that the size of the industrial capital stock in 1945 was negligible, an approximate value for the industrial capital stock for 1950 of 411 million lek at 1971 prices is obtained. Given the rapid rate of growth of the capital stock since 1950 and its small size at the time, the errors involved in the above assumptions are unlikely to distort the direction of the actual change in the capital–labour ratio or, probably, even to greatly exaggerate its scale. The results of the calculation are shown in Table 3.2, and leave no doubt

TABLE 3.2 *Industrial capital stock*

	1950	*1955*	*1960*	*1963*	*1970*	*1973*	*1975*
Industrial capital stock (million leks at 1971 prices)	411	1,589	3,507	4,678	10,858	14,598	17,057
Capital-labour ratio (000 leks/man)	25	55	73	70	102	120	128
Capital–output ratio	0.89	1.25	1.26	1.38	1.53	1.52	1.58

Source: see Appendix C.

about there being an increase in the industrial capital–labour ratio over twenty-five years.[9]

Two tests of consistency with the Stalinist development strategy remain. First, the priority law requires that group A production be growing faster than group B; and, second, the share of heavy industry in global industrial production must be increasing over time. Heavy industry is here taken, in the Albanian context, to include the following branches: oil, coal, chrome, copper, ferro-nickel, electric energy, engineering, chemicals, and construction materials. The rising share of heavy industrial output in gross industrial product for various years is shown in Table 3.3.

TABLE 3.3 *Share of heavy industry in global industrial output at 1971 prices*

1938	*1950*	*1965*	*1970*	*1973*
%	%	%	%	%
19.4	20.6	26.0	38.4	40.5

Source: 30 vjet Shqipëri socialiste (hereafter, *30 vjet*) Tirana, 1974, p. 65.

Before the Second World War, Albania was the most backward country in Europe, with a per capita industrial production of about $8 a year. There were only 150 industrial enterprises in the country, and of these almost half employed fewer than ten workers. The contribution of industrial production to net material product was only about 4½ per cent in 1938. Wartime damage to the infrastructure (roads, bridges, and dwellings) was heavy, but raw materials production capacity was enlarged: output of oil and chrome increased, and the extraction of natural gas, copper, iron, and manganese was begun. Consequently, when the PLA – or, as it was then known, the Communist Party of Albania – came to power it saw the establishment of manufacturing industry as the key to the modernization of the Albanian economy. The PLA's ideology of industrialization was fully in accord with the prevailing Marxist–Leninist doctrine that socialism can not be built without a strong industrial sector, and that this must be developed as rapidly as possible. Thus, at the first Congress of the CPA, which was held in November 1948, it was decided that the Party's

> fundamental economic objective was to raise the country from its profound backwardness, through a vigorous development of the forces of production.
>
> The essence of this task was the socialist industrialization, and the

electrification, of the country. The absolute necessity for industrialization was dictated by the need to create an entirely new material–technical base for the people's economy. . . . Socialist industrialization had to be carried out at a rapid rate, within the shortest possible time so as to overcome the backwardness inherited from the past, to ensure the independent development of the economy, and to achieve an appreciable rise in the material and cultural level of the working masses.[10]

The PLA leadership had, even earlier, turned its attention to the need for foreign aid in implementing its industrialization strategy. In his report to the Fourth Plenum of the PLA Central Committee on 17 October 1945, Enver Hoxha noted that both Yugoslavia and the Soviet Union had agreed to provide Albania with credit, but warned against the danger of failure to pay back the loans at the agreed time: 'If we do not improve the economic sector, our obligations to our people and to the states with which we have entered trade agreements will cause us to become politically dependent. We should not forget this: we have had a bitter past.'[11] Further on, the report refers to Albania's oil deposits, and planned Soviet assistance in their exploitation: 'oil is our main resource, and interests everybody. Of course, in this vital sector we will rely on the help of the Soviet Union, but we will consider the interest of our country first.'

Thus, Enver Hoxha's preference for political independence in the matter of economic development had been made clear. However, the PLA leadership was divided on the development issue, as is indicated by the relationship that developed between Albania and Yugoslavia and the signing of an agreement in November 1946 which would have effectively incorporated the Albanian economy into the Yugoslav Federation. But when the split between Belgrade and Moscow became clear in 1948, Hoxha was able to use Stalin's hatred of Tito to assist him in purging the pro-Yugoslav wing of the PLA, led by Koçi Xoxe.

As Table 3.4 below shows, aid received by Albania may be estimated at 147.5 million new leks over the years 1945–8;[12] some of this came from UNRRA – $23.6 million, of which the United States provided $20.4 million[13] – but the larger part was provided by Yugoslavia. Although the aid is measured as a surplus of Yugoslav deliveries over imports, Hoxha argued in October 1948 that in fact the aid had come via Yugoslavia from the Soviet Union. He gave his sources as Molotov and Stalin: 'When it came to economic matters, Molotov said, "the Soviet Union will unsparingly help the Albanian people to rebuild their economy, but this help will be given through Yugoslavia, purely for reasons of foreign policy". Comrade Stalin repeated this to us when we went to Moscow.'[14]

It is clear that, from Hoxha's viewpoint, close economic ties with

TABLE 3.4 *Total Albanian trade at 1971 domestic prices (millions of leks)*

	Albanian exports	*Albanian imports*	*Trade deficit*
1945	2	7	5
1946	7.5	8	0.5
1947	19	121	102
1948	33	73	40
1949	24	52	28
1950	26	88	62
1951	37	159	122
1952	53	128	75
1953	45	161	116
1954	41	104	63
1955	52	172	120
1956	75	156	81
1957	117	214	97
1958	117	315	198
1959	136	342	206
1960	212	353	141
1961	211	314	103
1962	178	281	103
1963	209	308	99
1964	256	422	166
1965	270	469	199
1966	303	512	209
1967	317	523	206
1968	360	535	175
1969	368	661	293
1970	431	687	256

Source: See Appendix C.

Yugoslavia were incompatible with his development strategy for Albania, and the Albanian economy came to rely mainly on the Soviet Union and other members of Comecon for aid after 1948.

THE ALBANIAN EXPERIENCE, 1951–1965

The PLA at its Second Congress had set ambitious targets for the First Five-year Plan (1951–5). The average annual rate of growth of total industrial production was planned to be 27.7 per cent, comprising an increase in the production of the means of production of 31 per cent per annum, and an average annual increase of 26.5 per cent in the output of consumer goods. The priority sectors were mining and the food and light industries, Albania's rich mineral reserves accounting for the huge projected increases in producer goods output.

At the Fifth Plenum of the Central Committee of the PLA convened on 1 March 1953, several days after Stalin's death – it was disclosed that the economic plan for 1952 had only been 'realized in general'. The greatest failures occured in agriculture, and as the planned increases in agricultural activity had not been forthcoming, raw materials required for the industrial sector were in short supply, with consequent implications for the output of consumer goods in particular. Under these circumstances, the decision of the Fifth Plenum to increase plan targets for 1953 was surprising. On the other hand, it must be recalled that the plans of other Comecon countries were also revised upwards as a consequence of a meeting of party leaders at Hollohaza, and even though Albania's First Five-year Plan targets had not been ratified until March 1952, it remains possible that subsequent upward revisions were a result of further Soviet pressure.

Enver Hoxha has argued[15] that, with the death of Stalin, the Soviet leadership began to apply pressure on the Albanians to reduce their emphasis on industrialization and devote more attention to the development of agriculture. Of particular interest are Malenkov's and Mikoyan's alleged statements on the state of Albanian agriculture:

'Your peasants are short of food, have no oxen, have no flocks, have not even a chicken (only they know how they had counted the chickens of Albania!), let alone other things of prime necessity . . . .' 'Your economic situation is bad; your agriculture is in a miserable state; you have less livestock than before the war; you import 20 per cent of your bread grain; the collectivization is proceeding slowly; the peasantry is not convinced about the collectivization. You are exploiting the peasants. Financial matters are going badly with you. You do not know how to conduct trade,' the Armenian prattled.[16]

Hoxha's sarcasm notwithstanding, he makes no attempt at a specific refutation of these criticisms.

While Soviet pressure was probably influential in soon changing Albanian economic policy, a realignment of planning priorities in favour of agriculture and consumption was probably inevitable at this time. Ideologically inspired plans would have little meaning if they could not be fulfilled and would ultimately have been damaging, by prolonging the vicious circle of shortages into which the Albanian economy had been plunged. A reduced emphasis on industrialization was heralded at the Eighth Plenum of the Central Committee of the PLA on 24 December 1953. In his report to the plenum of the Central Committee of the PLA on 24 December 1953, Hoxha stated that, of the 14,330 million (old) leks invested in construction during the plan period so far, only 2,534 million leks had been allocated for agricultural projects. He further noted that, for the 1951–5 period as a whole, failure to design projects properly had led to an underestimation of the cost by 14,000 million leks. His awareness of the inflationary pressures resulting from the disproportionate development implied by the plan is made clear in the following passage from the report:

> The large number of workers, averaging nearly 26,000 a year, needed for our investments, the large quantities of materials used in construction and in the feeding and clothing of the workers and their families, have reduced the quantities of consumer goods on the market, while the circulation of money has been increased and the necessary manpower for agriculture has been reduced.[17]

Following a discussion of the failure of various sectors to meet their plans, Hoxha noted the adverse implications of the economic situation for Albania's balance of payments and announced several changes in the targets of the Five-year Plan. The distribution of investment was altered so that the major part was now to go to agriculture and more than before to the consumer goods branches. The time horizon for the construction of some projects was extended, while other planned projects were cancelled; the arrears of delivery quotas for grain and other agricultural products for the period 1949–52 were cancelled; the tax burden on the agricultural community was lightened; and retail prices of domestically produced farm implements were decreased. Further, it was decided that the number of employees in the state apparatus would be reduced and that the 300 state enterprises and 17 central directorates in existence at the time would be amalgamated into 171 enterprises with no central directorates.

Given the irrationality of the pre-1954 targets for industrial production, it is perhaps a reflection of the relative success of the December 1953 measures that over the five-year period 1951–5 global industrial production was reported to have increased at an average annual rate of 22.8 per cent, as against the 27.7 per cent originally planned, while the annual rate of growth of consumer goods output, at 24.3 per cent, exceeded the 20.7 per cent average annual increase in producer goods production.[18]

Thus, if one looks at reported actual developments in relation to the Stalinist development rules, although the capital–labour ratio more than doubled (Table 3.2), thanks partly to imports of equipment, the rate of growth of group B output was greater than that of group A. Further, the share of heavy industrial output in global industrial production fell by 10 per cent.[19] In other words the backward nature of the Albanian economy did not permit a rapid expansion of heavy industry at the expense of the agricultural sector. On the other hand, the realignment of investment priorities in 1953, combined with a rapid rate of economic growth, provided the basis on which later five-year-plans could build in accordance with the Stalinist strategy.

The major directives of the Second Five-year Plan (1956–60) approved at the Third Congress of the PLA were modest compared with those of the First Five-year Plan, although it was again intended that group A production would increase at a somewhat more rapid rate than the production of consumer goods. Thus, global industrial production was to increase at an average annual rate of 14 per cent, 14.8 per cent by group A and 13.5 per cent by group B.

In direct contrast to the first two years of the First Five-year Plan, 1956 and, particularly, 1957 were good years for the Albanian economy. In the latter year, global industrial production rose by 26 per cent and global agricultural production by 15 per cent. There was then an upward revision of plan targets in February 1958, possibly based on these successes, though the official reason was the discovery of 'internal accumulation and reserves'. Thus, the target for the average annual rate of growth of global industrial output was raised from 14 to 17.5 per cent over the five-year period, the new rates for group A and group B becoming, respectively, 20 and 15.8 per cent.

In his address to the Fourth Congress of the PLA, it is not surprising that Mehmet Shehu compared the results of the Second Five-year Plan with the targets set by the Third Congress, for, while these were largely over-fulfilled, the levels anticipated in 1958 were not attained. Global industrial production had in fact increased at an average annual rate of nearly 17 per cent, output of means of production 18 per cent, and consumer goods output 16 per cent.[20] Although the share of heavy industrial output in the total was only 4.7 per cent higher than it had been in 1950, this represented an increase in the volume of output of heavy industry of over 16 per cent a year over the five years since 1955.[21] Finally, the capital–labour ratio had risen further by 33 per cent over the five year period.

In many respects, the Albanian Second Five-year Plan represented a victory for the Stalinist development strategy. During the early 1950s it had become clear that, while the ideology recognizes no limitations on the rate of industrial growth, even large free gifts of foreign plant and equipment are of little immediate use if the basic sectors including domestic agriculture do not provide the raw materials for industry. To a certain extent, the PLA appears to have realized this when it set the more modest targets in 1956; and, although revolutionary enthusiasm seemed to take over again briefly in 1958, the fact that the achievements of the plan were midway between the original and the revised targets suggests that they were around the upper limits set by the possibilities of the Albanian economy.

By February 1961, when the Fourth Congress convened, Albanian relations with the Soviet Union had deteriorated almost to the point of rupture. The conflict between Albania and the Soviet Union had become public in 1960 at the Peking meeting of the World Federation of Trade Unions, when, for the first time, Albania openly supported China in its arguments against the Soviet Union; though diplomatic relations between the Soviet Union and Albania were not finally severed until 3 December 1961. In the intervening period, credits of about $132 million which had been promised to Albania for the Third Five-year Plan by Comecon members were cancelled, Soviet experts left Albania, the Soviet naval base at Vlorë was dismantled, and China provided $123 million in grant-aid and credits to replace those withdrawn by the Soviet Union and its allies.

Several factors that probably determined the direction of Albanian involvement in the Sino-Soviet dispute may be noted. It is clear that the Albanian leadership was disturbed by Khrushchev's denunciation of Stalin, Hoxha believing that the framework established by Stalin for socialist construction represented the only valid Marxist–Leninist line. The Soviet rapprochement with Yugoslavia in the late 1950s may have appeared to Tirana to pose a threat to Albanian independence, and Hoxha had already demonstrated his nationalistic tendencies in the dispute with Xoxe and Tito. In addition to these more compelling reasons to choose alliance with China, the PLA leadership's desire for independence in determining development policy would undoubtedly be more easily reconciled with alliance with China than the USSR, and Soviet ideas of 'integration' through Comecon. Further, while China could scarcely be expected to be as lavish with aid as the Soviet Union had been, the small size of the Albanian economy made it likely that the drain on China's resources of aid that was significant to Albania would be small in Chinese eyes. Further, it was not unlikely that China would provide more heavy industrial plant than the Soviet Union had wished to do (see below).

There can be no doubt that Albania's decision to break with the Soviet Union meant that Albania would be turning her back on – so far – consistently high levels of aid from Comecon. The reasons for Comecon's persistent generosity in the face of a high probability that the debt would turn bad are unknown, and Wiles's conclusion that 'Albania's performance can only be described as a remarkable diplomatic achievement'[22] would be hard to dispute. The scale of aid may be approximately indicated by Albania's foreign trade deficit, and this deficit had accumulated rapidly (see Table 3.4). Given the relative insignificance of invisibles, it seems reasonable to use the visible balance of payments deficit as a surrogate for economic aid. Table 3.4 shows that aid to Albania fell from 116 million leks in 1953 to 63 million leks in the following year. Hoxha's memoirs give the impression that the Soviet leadership used dissatisfaction with Albania's development strategy to reduce the level of aid requested by Tirana:

For several days on end we battled with Mikoyan, who set to work with his pruning shears. In order to reject our requests for the development of industry, which were modest enough, but on which we insisted, he and his comrades, as usual, repeated the same old refrain: 'Why do you need industry? Don't you see the state of your countryside?'[23]

On the other hand, following these initial difficulties with the post-Stalin regime in Moscow, aid flowed to Albania with renewed vigour. Thus, whereas the Albanian cumulative trade deficit was 545 million leks for the years 1947–53, for the shorter period 1954–9 it was significantly greater, at 765 million leks. Albania was released from repayment of all its debts to the Soviet Union in April 1957, and a further credit of 300 million roubles was offered for the Third Five-year Plan.[24] But when relations between Albania and the Soviet Union deteriorated this offer was withdrawn, and all trade between the two countries ceased after 1961.

Some impression of the influence of Comecon aid on Albanian industrial development may be gained from a consideration of the number and nature of new industrial enterprises commissioned in Albania between 1947 and 1961, all of which must have depended upon imported equipment. Of 37 new enterprises, 8 belonged to branches of mining and heavy industry, while the remainder were in the light or food industry branches.[25] This is consistent with the tendency for Comecon to stress the Albanian potential to supply agricultural products to the rest of the area; but the composition of aid may have been less than ideal from an Albanian viewpoint. The PLA leadership may have felt qualms, similar to those later given vigorous expression by Romania, that the country was being designated as a source of primary products for the Comecon area.

Finally, it may be noted that, from a purely political standpoint, the popularity of the Albanian regime might well be raised by appeals to anti-Slav feelings among the population; and the fact that the PLA had come to power without direct Soviet intervention suggested that Soviet influence in the country would not be necessary to keep the party in power. There is even evidence to suggest that the reverse might be true of Hoxha's own ability to retain power. According to Pano, the 'Soviets . . . appear to have been involved in the preparation of an armed uprising by disaffected elements within Albania.'[26]

The Fourth Congress had ratified a planned increase in global industrial production of 52 per cent over the period of the Third Five-year Plan (1961–5), group A output being planned to increase by 54 per cent and group B output by 50 per cent.[27] But when it became clear that the Soviet Union would rescind all projected credits, the PLA convened a Plenum of its Central Committee which, on 1 July 1961, issued a decision entitled 'On measures which must be taken for the further strengthening of the regime of the economy'. The essence of this document was an appeal to all Albanians to economize wherever possible: ministries were asked to make sure that unplanned losses within enterprises did not occur; workers were exhorted to use their equipment with the utmost care and to think of ways in which the return on capital might be raised in production. It was stressed that the volume of exports would have to rise if Albania were to be able to buy the machines and equipment that it needed from abroad. This was probably the first statement issued by the PLA that indicated an awareness that the economic situation was going to be affected by the change in alliance from the Soviet Union to China. It has been claimed that, as a consequence of cost reduction methods employed in 1961, 1,700 million leks were saved; and this figure represents 6 per cent of the state budget for 1961.[28] The year's plan for global industrial production was over-fulfilled by 5 per cent, and gross agricultural output rose by 22 per cent over that of 1960 – which had, however, been a rather bad year.[29]

External pressure on the Albanian economy increased in 1962, when several Eastern European states cancelled promised credits. Imports were cut back during 1961–3 and the trade deficit fell to only about half its earlier – peak – level (see Table 3.4). However, it seems that the major problems faced by the Albanian economy resulted not only from cut-backs in foreign credits, and therefore in 'free' imports of goods, but also from an inability to generate sufficient 'disembodied technical progress', for no country in Europe had fewer experts than Albania in 1962. Moreover, the massive education drive undertaken after the Second World War was severely hampered when Albanian students in Comecon countries were forced to return home, their scholarships rescinded. There was little doubt that Chinese experts would be made available to replace the Soviet advisors, but the problems caused in China by the 'Great Leap Forward' cannot have helped in this context.

More significantly, however, the change from Soviet to Chinese technology meant that any projects left unfinished in 1961 would take longer to complete than had been planned. Of the nine major construction projects completed in 1961, only one, a briquette factory, actually contributed an increase in industrial capacity. In 1962, only 6 of the 23 largest new construction projects reported as completed could be said to contribute to the Albanian industrial capital stock. It was not until 1965 that industrial enterprises comprised the majority of new projects commissioned.

The estimates of the capital–labour ratio in Albanian industry (Table 3.2) provide further evidence of the difficulties faced by the economy in introducing new equipment and new technology during the Third Five-year Plan: the ratio actually fell between 1960 and 1963. It is not possible to determine with accuracy at what point the capital–labour ratio began to increase again, as the labour productivity changes required to calculate the industrial labour force for any time between 1963 and 1970 have not been published. Nor is it surprising that the change in industrial labour productivity over the period of the Third Five-year Plan has not been published, since a fall in labour productivity is ideologically inconceivable in a Stalinist economy.[30] A fall of some 12½ per cent in industrial labour productivity between 1960 and 1963, followed by an increase in global industrial production of only 14 per cent over the two years 1964–5, means that it is most unlikely that there was any increase in labour productivity in industry over the Five-year Plan period. It must remain a question whether the fall, or medium-term stagnation, of labour productivity and the reduction in the industrial capital–labour ratio reflected not only a hiatus in industrial investment and the 'normal' drift of labour from agriculture to industry, but also a deliberate further shift of labour from agriculture to industry in an attempt to compensate for the reduction in the flow of new foreign capital.

In aggregate terms, the Third Five-year Plan was a failure. The continuing priority for industry may be judged by the 97 per cent fulfilment of industrial targets under the Plan, implying a 50 per cent rise in global industrial output, with global agricultural output increasing by a mere 22 per cent over the period (the plan having called for an increase of 72 per cent).[31] The increase in real income of the population also fell short of the plan target. Notwithstanding Albanian industry's failure to meet all its targets, however, the detailed evidence indicates a remarkable advance in industrial production, given a good start by the 22 per cent rise in agricultural output in the one year, 1961. This was particularly important in the 'autarkic' conditions of the Albanian economy after the break with the Soviet Union, when agriculture had to supply an even greater proportion of the inputs to industry than had been the case in the past. Just as the negative experience of the First Five-year Plan revealed the difficulties involved in applying the Stalinist development strategy to a developing economy with a backward agricultural sector, so did experience under the Third Five-year Plan underline Albania's heavy dependence on foreign aid if rapid growth of industrial capacity and labour productivity was to be achieved.

In general terms, one can characterize the period up to 1965 as one of rapid but erratic growth for the Albanian economy. All three Five-year Plans were revised in midstream as a consequence either of external factors or of realization that the original plan had been too ambitious. Industrial development was similarly rapid but erratic, and although high growth rates were achieved in all sectors, the weight of heavy industry output in the total did not change significantly between 1950 and 1965 (see Table 3.3).

Several reasons may be advanced for the failure of the Albanian government to achieve, up to 1965, its stated aim of heavy industrialization at all costs. First, it has already been suggested that Soviet plant and equipment installed in Albania may have contributed to the development of food processing, light industry, and some extractive industries rather than to mineral processing or capital goods manufacturing. Secondly, although Albanian leaders and economists stressed – and continue to stress – the need to develop heavy industry at a more rapid rate than any other sector throughout the period of socialist construction, a specific sectoral strategy for implementing this goal was never actually put forward. Third, the chronic lack of expert managers and technicians, and of skilled workers, meant that it would be easier to achieve significant expansion in those areas of industry – such as food-processing and handicrafts – that had always existed in Albania and did not demand the manipulation of modern technology.

Finally, it seems reasonable to argue that the failure of the heavy industrialization programme made the Albanian leadership aware that acceptance of the 'law of priority of the production of the means of production' may be a statement of an economic goal, but certainly does not represent a precise development strategy. The strategy implied by the 'scientific–technical revolution', which was launched in 1967, was arguably the first attempt made by the PLA to differentiate between the various branches of heavy industry, recognizing the importance of the Albanian economy's resource endowment.

THE SCIENTIFIC–TECHNICAL REVOLUTION AND SELF-RELIANCE

The third Plenum of the Central Committee of the PLA was convened on 13 October 1967. The speakers at the Plenum stressed the importance of a thorough reorganization of the engineering industry, conceding that earlier attempts had failed (see below), and outlined, for the first time, a fairly precise development strategy for Albanian industry. Albania's conflicts with first Yugoslavia and then the Soviet Union were cited as important reasons why the PLA should make every attempt to ensure that Albania's economic development took place with the greatest possible reliance on the country's natural resources, and that the Albanian economy should one day be 'self-sufficient'. There seems little doubt that Albania's natural resource endowment was a crucial factor in convincing the PLA leadership that 'economic independence' within a relatively short period was a real possibility. It was decided that three branches of industry should be given priority, and developed as rapidly as possible: the electrical, chemical, and engineering industries.

The decision to use electricity as the economy's major source of energy was determined by the fact that Albania is a mountainous country with many rivers, providing an ideal basis for hydroelectric sites. Thus, while the construction of power stations involves high initial investment, running costs are low, and a large proportion of the construction costs would probably be borne by China. Further, the use of electricity would allow Albania to develop oil production, largely for export, thus potentially covering the running costs of the electricity branch out of foreign exchange earnings. Finally, the plan to provide every Albanian village with electricity – a goal achieved in 1971 – provided the PLA with a focal point for mass mobilization drives, and echoed Lenin's stress on electrification in the Soviet Union.

The importance of the chemical industry in the 'scientific–technical revolution' is also related to natural resource endowments. The extraction and processing of minerals for final use, both domestically and for export, requires the application of chemical-intensive technology, the chemical inputs often being available as part of the same resource base. Thus, as in the case for electricity, once the initial investment required for the construction of the relevant plants has been financed – again, using aid from China – the processes can be maintained very largely from domestic resources. The potential cost saving for industry promised by the use of organic synthetics, such as plastics, also provided an incentive to develop a strong chemical industry.

From the viewpoint of comparative advantage, the development of electric power and the chemical industry in Albania might arguably be justified – although the PLA was clearly not concerned with trade as a means of ensuring economic efficiency, since the drive for economic independence was seen as necessitating high priority also for an industry unlikely to be yet well suited to the conditions of the Albanian economy. But the motivation for giving the engineering industry priority is clear; if Albania could produce all the spare parts needed to service her current capital stock and, eventually, could produce the majority of additions to that stock, a large step towards 'economic independence' could have been taken. Self-sufficiency in agricultural products has always been a goal of the Albanian authorities, and even here the development of the engineering industry could be seen as a necessary contribution to raising the low level of productivity of farm labour and land.

It should be noted that the Albanian notion of self-sufficiency for the engineering industry implies heavy reliance on existing levels of technology. While information on world advances in scientific research might well become known to Albanian planners, the insistence that such advances should be incorporated into new plant using largely domestically available labour, production facilities, and expertise seems unrealistic (see below).

THE ALBANIAN ENGINEERING INDUSTRY

Towards the end of 1965, articles in the Albanian press began urging the engineering industry to increase the quantity and quality of its production by concentrating its capital stock and specializing its production, to make gains from economies of scale, and by developing such links as were possible between enterprises in the industry to facilitate co-operation in production. Although there is no evidence that any measures were taken at the time – and there may well have been some contrary developments, judging by the events of 1967 – the tactics of concentration, specialization, and co-operation were to prove important weapons in the attempted implementation of the 'scientific–technical revolution'.

The Albanian engineering industry is concerned with the production and repair of machine spare parts, various tools and equipment, and some consumer goods. In 1967 40 per cent of its output came from Tirana and the industry employed about 12,000 people. This then represented about 12 per cent of total employment in industry in Albania. The industry shared many of the problems common to the rest of the economy, such as emphasis on global indicators at the expense of assortment, considerable waste of resources, delays in obtaining inputs, and generally poor co-ordination of the production process. Technical inefficiency was a major problem. Thus, the quality of output was prejudiced from the beginning by the fact that poor-quality raw materials or, what is perhaps worse, steel of indeterminate quality (i.e., steel the quality of which has not been documented) was provided to the enterprise. Then, frequently the majority of the production processes of the enterprise had not been set out in detailed technological charts, but goods were produced with reference to an existing sample. Under these circumstances, it was almost impossible to ensure the standardization of output. Some measure of the extent of this particular problem is given by the fact that, of the 330 items produced in quantities greater than 100 units per year at one of the largest plants in Tirana, operational – or even pending – technological charts and accurate drawings of the final products existed for only 35, and when the output was produced, very little of it underwent the thermal or galvanic processing necessary to increase its life.

The uncoordinated nature of the engineering industry's development prior to 1967 is indicated by the fact that the industry then consisted of three large enterprises in Tirana and a series of small workshops located throughout the country; their output was not highly specialized, and production of enterprises under the control of the engineering sub-section of the Ministry of Industry and Mining represented only 61 per cent of the total output of engineering products in 1966.[32]

Thus, the first element in the reorganization of the industry was the concentration of its capital stock – mainly metal-cutting machine tools – in a small number of enterprises to make gains from economies of scale. But the attempts to do this were apparently resisted by enterprise directors, who allegedly wanted as many machines around them as possible, even if they were not in use, and – perhaps with some justification – feared 'that, once the machine left the enterprise, no one would know what had happened to it'.[33] However, following the Third Plenum, the concentration of metal-cutting equipment led to the establishment of several new enterprises and the expansion of some already in existence; and it was stated that, because machines that had previously been unused owing to the lack of qualified workers were reallocated more rationally, the capacity of the engineering industry was increased without significant additional investment or a reduction in the output of other sectors.

The second feature of the reorganized engineering industry, which could come about only as a consequence of concentration, was specialization of production. Attempts would be made to avoid 'unnecessary duplication in production', and to obtain the benefits of mass production wherever demand warranted it. The more common use of continuous production lines was expected to reduce costs owing to time lost in the setting up of machinery, or changing tools where production had previously been organized on a handicraft basis.

Finally, it should be noted that specialization was to be applied only with care to the education of cadres. Thus, Gambeta[34] notes the risk of producing 'professional idiots', and explains that both technical progress and socialism require 'polytechnically trained' cadres.

The third step in the reorganization of the engineering industry required increased co-operation between enterprises. This meant that, whenever certain goods could be produced with only capacity located in different enterprises, the relevant enterprises would enter into contractual agreements occupying a special place in the state plan. Thus, for example, a plant producing machinery may make arrangements for the use of thermal-processing or galvanizing equipment necessary for its production but available only at a nearby enterprise, which has the required equipment not operating at full capacity.

Finally, the 'scientific–technical revolution' laid great stress on the maximum exploitation of capacity in the engineering industry. According to PLA Central Committee Secretary, Xhafer Spahiu, this could be achieved only if the 'Party, Government and economic organs' made particular note of the following:

> the maximum exploitation of inventoried machinery and mechanisms, because there are various enterprises which do not utilize all their available machinery;
>
> the elimination of bottlenecks through partial reconstruction of various lines, units, and machinery aggregates so as to harmonize the productive capacity of various technological processes within the enterprise;
>
> the improved utilization of calendar time, by increasing the amount of actual working time between repairs. To this end, three-shift working or repair squads should be tried, as well as the preparation in advance of those spare parts that are more often damaged;
>
> the reduction of construction time and the mastering of the productive capacity of new projects is also of great importance in this direction.
>
> In addition, other ways and possibilities should be found and studied, according to the concrete conditions in each and every enterprise or branch of the economy.[35]

Thus, the most important feature of the planned reorganization of the engineering industry was an attempt to increase technical efficiency and levels of output by concentration, specialization, and co-operation without a heavy investment programme; and this was expected to be possible because of the extent of under-utilization of capacity up to 1967 owing to *ad hoc* allocation and lack of skilled workers. On the other hand, the engineering industry was not yet capable of producing sophisticated capital equipment, and had only one plant capable of producing spare parts (and other simple metal products). Thus, while the long-term aim of economic independence would be realized only through the import of more machinery than Albania could possibly finance from current exports, in the short term, it was decided to attempt to become self-sufficient in spare parts production as a first step.

The problem of integrating world advances in technology into Albanian production processes has already been mentioned. The 'scientific–technical revolution' attempted to take it into account with a call for improvements in the organization of technological research in the country, particularly at enterprise level. Problems of technical progress are dealt with in enterprises by the enterprise's technological and design bureau, and any laboratories under its jurisdiction. The working methods of the bureau of the Tractor Spare Parts Factory have been cited in the press as an example for all to follow. In this plant,

> the engineers, technicians, and workers of the technological and design bureau go down to the production units and consult with the production workers before starting to plan and to establish the production technology for any given part. Later on the planners follow up the application of the technological process decided upon throughout the experimental stage and also during the stage of actual production. In this way the engineers and other workers of the bureau are in continual touch with every phase of studying, planning and experimenting, and production. In addition to facilitating and speeding up planning and to avoiding or minimizing possible mistakes, this method of working also helps safeguard the cadres from the dangers of technocracy and helps to forge close links between planning and production workers and vice versa. This method also helps to raise the technical standard of the workers, thus implementing Comrade Enver's teaching that 'practice aids theory and theory aids and guides practice'.[36]

While the emphasis on expert–worker relations was not an essential part of the 'scientific–technical revolution', this quotation indicates the extent to which the ideological campaigns permeated the Albanian economic literature of the time.

While the Albanian authorities were stressing the aims of 'self-reliance' and 'economic independence' which were to be promoted by the 'scientific–technical revolution' and, specifically, by reorganizing the capital goods industries and pursuing self-sufficiency in production of spare parts for capital equipment, both the physical capacity and the expertise necessary to produce industrial equipment were extremely limited in the mid-1960s – as, indeed, they still are today. If Stalin's demand for the 'perfection of socialist production on the basis of higher techniques' was to be met over a reasonable time, by steadily raising the stock of capital available to each worker, imports of equipment would long remain essential and in the near future would exceed what could be paid for by exports without depressing Albanian living standards – or even, probably, if such a sacrifice *were* to be made. There is, in fact, little doubt that the value of Chinese aid to Albania increased steadily between 1965 and 1973; but it is interesting to note that the Albanian press has never explicitly acknowledged this fact.

THE PERFORMANCE OF THE PRIORITY INDUSTRIES

Before considering the performance of Albanian industry as a whole since the call for a 'scientific–technical revolution', an examination of the performance of the three priority industries can highlight some of the predictable advantages and disadvantages of the Albanian development strategy. Some figures for the output of the electicity, chemical, and engineering industries are given in Tables 3.5 – 3.7. It is not surprising that the industry facing the most difficulties since 1967 has been the engineering industry, representing the most ambitious part of the industrialization programme. By 1973 the industry had raised the output of spare parts by 310 per cent over the 1965 level,[37] and the ratio of domestic production to imports had risen as shown in Table 3.8. Given that the engineering industry fulfilled its target of doubling output during the Fifth Five-year Plan period (1971–5), it is possible that the planned proportions in this table were met or even exceeded;

TABLE 3.5 *Production of electrical energy (million kwh)*

	1938	*1950*	*1960*	*1970*	*1973*
Total	9	21	200	943	1,603
Hydro source	0	–	125	451	1,127
Thermal source	9	–	68	476	476

Source: 30 vjet p.75. Discrepancies are those of the original table.

TABLE 3.6 *Chemical industry production*

	1960	*1965*	*1970*	*1973*
Total (million leks at 1971 prices)	14	36	251	326
Phosphate fertilizer ('000 tons)	0	0	110	110
Nitrate fertilizer ('000 tons)	0	0	76	106
Calcium hydroxide ('000 tons)	0	0	11	21
Caustic soda ('000 tons)	0	0	13	16
Oil and enamel paints ('000 tons)	0	0.5	1	2

Source: 30 vjet. p. 85.

TABLE 3.7 *Engineering industry production* (million leks at 1971 prices)

	1950	*1960*	*1970*	*1973*
Total	19	103	688	1,239
Machines and equipment	0	2	152	274
Spare parts	4	24	149	238
Consumer goods*	15	77	387	727

Source: 30 vjet, p.81.

* Residual, not specified in source.

TABLE 3.8 *Ratio of domestic production to imports of spare parts*

1965	37:63	1973	61:39
1970	52:48	1974 (plan)	(62:38)
1971	53:47	1975 (plan)	(68:32)
1972	58:42		

Source: Probleme ekonomike, no. 3, 1974, p.4.

and, according to the indicators of the Sixth Five-year Plan (1976–80), Albania should have been 95 per cent self-sufficient in spare parts by 1980.

However, notwithstanding the success of the industry in terms of increased levels of output and import substitution, efficiency has remained a problem. Thus, in 1970 one of the largest enterprises in the industry lost an estimated 8 per cent of its production through unexcused worker absenteeism (though still fulfilling its production plan), and in 1971 the industry as a whole failed to meet its plan for input of labour-time, with an 11 per cent deficit for the same reason. Global output per man in the industry, computed at current prices, has also shown an apparently disappointing development. Between 1967, the first year of the 'scientific–technical revolution', and 1971 the figure actually fell, from 35,300 leks per man to 27,300 leks.[38] The limited evidence provided by Table 3.1 above suggests that this fall ran counter to the trend for industry as a whole. On the other hand, while output per man in the engineering industry remains below the level of other sectors – probably as a consequence of problems arising from lack of expertise, misallocation of labour, and disguised unemployment – the share of the industry's production in global industrial output rose from 5.7 to 9.8 per cent between 1965 and

1970,[39] while its share in total capital investment in machines and equipment rose less, from 36.7 per cent in 1961–5 to 38.6 per cent in 1966–9.[40] This is probably accounted for – at least in part – by the increased production made possible by concentration of capital and an improved use of capacity; and it is at least possible that this concentration also reduced the amount of duplication in the global output figure (thus, the actual fall in labour productivity would be overstated), and/or that increasing series production was accompanied by price reductions (with similar effect).

ALBANIAN INDUSTRIAL PERFORMANCE, 1966–1977

Although more optimistic than its predecessor, the Fourth Five-year Plan (1966–70) called for an increase of only between 50 and 54 per cent in global industrial production, representing an average annual rate of growth of 8.7 per cent, with group A production increasing at a rate of 10.8 per cent against 6.2 per cent for group B. In the event, the plan targets were significantly exceeded, global industrial production in 1970 being 83 per cent above that recorded for 1965, while group A recorded an average annual rise of 15.8 per cent. The production of industrial consumer goods rose by an average 9.5 per cent per annum.[41] As Table 3.3 above shows, the share of heavy industrial output in global industrial production increased from 26 per cent in 1965 to nearly 38.5 per cent in 1970, the largest increase registered in any five years of Albanian history.

On the other hand, although the data for 1963 and 1970 in Table 3.1 above suggest that labour productivity probably rose over the (shorter) plan period, no official figure has ever been published. If, indeed, productivity rose, this is surprising, since only in the reported results of the Third Five-year Plan, when productivity fell, had this indicator not been made available previously. In tabling his report on the plan to the PLA's Sixth Congress, Mehmet Shehu did not even mention industrial labour productivity; and it was left to Enver Hoxha to concede that this part of the plan had not been realized, though he did not provide any statistics:

> The successes already achieved in raising the productivity of labour in our economy are not small. But during the Fourth Five-year Plan period there were some deficiencies, with planned targets for the increase of productivity not achieved. As a consequence of the slow rate of increase of the productivity of labour, the increase of industrial production was due almost entirely to increasing the number of workers above the planned limit. This caused a disproportion between the increase of production and the wages fund.[42]

There is thus some conflict of evidence, but most probably the growth of labour productivity in industry during this period was insignificant; and, paradoxically, this and the large increase in total industrial output may have a common cause. Table 3.4 shows Albanian imports of 2,918 million leks in the years 1966–70, against 1,794 million in the previous quinquennium and corresponding trade deficits of 1,139 million leks and 670 million. There was thus a large increase in imports of capital and in industrial capacity, the latter probably on a scale that required a large expansion of the industrial labour force, while – because of lack of skills and for other reasons – the enlarged capital stock still could not be exploited to full capacity. It is at least possible that Hoxha's report could more reasonably have been put in the form that it was the increase in the labour force necessary to man the new industrial projects completed during the plan period that led to the low rise in labour productivity – a hypothesis to which the discussion of productivity problems in the engineering industry (above) lends some support, as does the faster rise in the industrial capital – output ratio between 1960 and 1970 than in either the previous or the subsequent five years (see Tables 3.1 and 3.2).

Nevertheless, the change from an over-simple 'macroeconomic' approach to the Stalinist development strategy of priority for heavy industry – with a rather *ad hoc* determination of sectoral growth targets and investment allocations – to one that included a 'micro-economic' concentration on those branches appropriate to Albania's resource endowment, and on improving efficiency within them, is reflected in extremely rapid growth of output of the three priority branches between 1965 and 1970. The annual rates of some 47.5 per cent and 25.5 per cent recorded in the chemical and engineering industries, respectively, were higher than those in any other branch of Albanian industry, while electric power recorded the fifth highest average annual rate of growth at over 21 per cent.[43]

The Sixth Congress of the PLA approved a target of around 11.6 billion leks for the value of global industrial production in 1975, an increase of 61–66 per cent over 1970, while group A production was to rise by 78–83 per cent and consumer goods production by 40–44 per cent.

Statistics published in 1974 suggested that these Fifth Five-year Plan targets would probably be met. Global industrial production in 1973 was slightly above the level that would have been implied by a steady expansion at the average annual rate of 10.3 per cent required for the whole plan period, and the planned split between group A and group B production was being virtually achieved.[44] However, from the beginning of 1974 it seems clear that the Albanian authorities felt that the industrial output targets of the plan might be beyond the economy's grasp. The 1974 annual plan called for an increase of 8 per cent in global industrial production, and 7.3 per cent was achieved. The 1975 plan was even more pessimistic, calling for an increase of only 4.4 per cent, and the outturn was a 4 per cent rise.[45]

Thus, for the Fifth Five-year Plan period as a whole, global industrial production had risen by some 51–52 per cent, and it had also shown a tendency for the pattern to change in a direction contrary to that originally planned. Whereas the increase in the production of industrial consumer goods was 45 per cent, and thus exceeded the plan target mentioned above, group A production was only 57 per cent above the 1970 level (against 78–83 per cent planned). Over the last two years of the plan period, 1974 and 1975, the annual rate of growth of group B production even slightly exceeded that of group A (12.4 and 12.1 per cent, respectively).

Other changes in the nature of Albania's industrial development at some stage in 1973 or 1974 are indicated by the increases in labour productivity and the changes in the capital–labour and capital–output ratios registered by Albanian industry during the Fifth Five-year Plan. Between 1970 and 1973 there was an 18 per cent rise in labour productivity, though the capital stock appears to have grown relatively slowly – by about the same percentage as in the earlier, slack investment years, 1960–3. However, from 1970 to 1973 the tendency for the industrial capital–output ratio to rise seems to have been temporarily checked. In other words, industrial capital productivity appears to have stabilized or even to have risen very slightly. This suggests an improved utilization of capacity, and that some of the labour misallocation problems of the earlier years had been solved. Of course, the increased numbers of experts and skilled workers forthcoming over time should also have contributed to increased efficiency of production. However, during 1974–5 industrial capital productivity again fell, even though the growth of the capital stock did not apparently accelerate very significantly, and labour productivity rose by only 2.5 per cent despite a relatively modest increase in the industrial labour force (see Table 3.1).

The absence of any official Albanian analysis of the change in industrial development experienced halfway through the Fifth Five-year Plan – its existence as such is not even acknowledged – renders an explanation difficult. However, on the basis of the available evidence some tentative conclusions are possible. The major source of data on the problem is Enver Hoxha's *Reflections on China*,[46] which purports to be a political diary covering the period 1962–77. Since the published work is officially designated as 'Extracts from the political diary', there seems no reason to doubt the authenticity of the work. Indeed, the noticeable lack of information on 1974 – a year of extensive purges – lends credence to the veracity of the source.

Hoxha's first complaint about Chinese aid came on 9 December 1970, when he noted that the Chinese Deputy Minister of Energy had informed her near-opposite number Rahman Hanku that the Chinese would be unable to complete the 'Mao Tse-tung' hydroelectric power station on time, and that the Fierza power station could not be built on the projected site. When Hanku informed her that her arguments were unfounded, she recanted. Hoxha entered his first warning: 'Despite our friendship, we must be vigilant.'

The next relevant entry does not appear until 30 September 1972, when Hoxha discovers that the Chinese have not yet themselves procured the technical equipment that they had promised to supply for the Elbasan metallurgical combine. 'This presents many dangers for us. We shall see what develops.'

The first sign of a concrete reduction in aid came on 15 October of the same year, when the Chinese ambassador informed Hoxha that 'certain requests connected with the problems of our perspective plan for 1975–1980, and concretely about increasing the capacity for smelting ferro-nickel, the construction of the Koman hydro-power station, and the extension of the Balsh thermal power station'[47] would not be fulfilled.

On 13 March 1973 Hoxha recorded in his diary that Albania had been experiencing difficulties as a result of the tardiness of Chinese deliveries 'for a long time'. In the light of this evidence, the downward revision in the Five-year Plan implied by the low 1974 target for global industrial production may be explained by the PLA's possible anticipation of the reduction in aid. Mehmet Shehu's statement, at the Seventh Congress of the PLA, that the failure of the industrial projects to be completed on time had caused the economy problems, is consistent with this line of argument.

The development of Albanian trade at this time also suggests that there may have been a short-lived attempt to expand trade with the capitalist West (see Table 3.9), which could have been intended to compensate in part for any reduction in aid-financed supplies of equipment from China. Moreover, the 15 and 17 per cent annual increases in total exports in 1973 and 1974 were far above the 5.5 and 11 per cent increases originally planned.[48]

It remains to be noted that if – as seems most probable – an expected, and later actual, reduction in aid from China was the major factor producing a change in the industrial development strategy during the Fifth Five-year Plan, the reaction was very different from that

TABLE 3.9 *Albanian trade with 'developed capitalist' partners (millions of dollars)*

		Imports f.o.b.	*Exports* c.i.f.			*Imports* f.o.b.	*Exports* c.i.f.
1973	I	7	6	1975	I	26	15
	II	12	6		II	30	18
	III	15	7		III	15	19
	IV	10	12		IV	15	20
1974	I	12	9	1976	I	9	10
	II	26	15		II	11	14
	III	22	19		III	10	8
	IV	21	17				

Source: M.C. Kaser, 'Trade and Aid in the Albanian Economy', in Joint Economic Committee, US Congress, *East European Economies post-Helsinki,* Washington DC, 1977.

following the break with the Soviet Union in 1961. On this later occasion, the light and food industries continued to receive inputs permitting them to expand at more than the planned rates, while the growth of group A output slackened, and there was an export drive to the capitalist West as part of a more general expansion of exports from 1973 to 1975.

Thus, there appears to have been a temporary shift away from the Stalinist development strategy. But that the policy shift was only temporary was made clear when the Minister of Trade, the Minister of Industry and Mining, and the Chairman of the State Planning Commission were all dismissed at some time towards the end of 1975 – that is, when Albania's trade turnover with the West was beginning to drop back towards the level of the early 1970s. A possible reason for these dismissals could be that there had been sharp differences within the PLA leadership over the nature of the response in 1973 to an expected reduction in aid. It is likely, given the consistent attempts to maintain Stalinist development policies since the very early days of the PLA's rule, that some members of the leadership would have argued for a continuation of the current policy even in the face of anticipated difficulties. In the event, this faction was overruled, but the output level and pattern of 1975 represented an even worse setback to the Five-year Plan than those of 1974. Even though trade turnover with all 'Western' countries roughly doubled between 1973 and 1975, it seems to have been inadequate to compensate for the less satisfactory trade and aid relations with China. The Fifth Five-year Plan was not realized in the priority sectors or over all. The policy of 'moderation' adopted in 1973 had failed, and its advocates suffered the political consequences.

The accusations levelled at the dismissed ministers at the PLA's Seventh Congress in November 1976 are not inconsistent with the above hypothesis. Thus, Shehu accused the former Chairman of the State Planning Commission, Kellezi, the former Minister of Industry and Mining, Theodhosi, 'and others in the economic sector' of sabotaging the oil industry; while Hoxha, in his report, blamed those purged for the failure to complete certain construction projects as well as for shortfalls in the (Five-year) plans of the oil, chromium, copper, coal, bread grain, and industrial crop sectors. Referring to the oil industry, Hoxha charged Kellezi and Theodhosi with using 'refined methods to disorient exploration' and mismanage the industry, with preventing the exploitation of new sources of oil and gas, and with using 'barbaric' methods for the exploitation of existing wells.

CONCLUSION

There are insufficient data available to allow the conclusion that the above scenario is correct in all details. However, an important point is clear: nearly thirty years of experience with the Stalinist development strategy, during which time the Albanian economy had achieved rates of economic growth unsurpassed elsewhere in Europe, did not guarantee its continued pursuit in the face of a reduction in the level of foreign aid. A possible reason for opposition to the policy within the PLA is that it has required a higher rate of domestic savings than some PLA leaders felt was equitable for the population to bear.

To the extent that the Albanian government has attempted to use aid for the development of heavy industry, Chinese aid appears to have been more appropriate than credit from Comecon. Thus, between 1962 and 1964 there were 12 new industrial enterprises commissioned, of which only 3 were heavy industrial (Chinese aid probably being employed during this period to complete projects begun prior to the changeover), while between 1965 and 1970 there were 41 new enterprises opened, of which 24 contributed to heavy industrial output.[50]

From a theoretical viewpoint, the adoption of the Stalinist development strategy by a developing economy – that is, the priority development of heavy industry with advances in technology provided by an ever-increasing capital–labour ratio – is likely to pose several problems. An attempt to begin the acceleration of industrial output when the agricultural sector is unable to supply the necessary raw materials will almost certainly fail unless a significant proportion of foreign credit is spent on the import of those materials. However, to the extent that the amount of disposable credit is limited, this must limit the development of new industrial capacity. Further, even if offers of credit are unlimited, the disproportions generated by leaving agriculture in a backward state will make the economy ever-increasingly dependant on foreign aid, with the political – and eventual economic – dysfunctions such a situation might imply. To some extent this problem may still beset the Albanian economy, although its impact was most severe during the First Five-year Plan.

Another problem inherent in the application of the Stalinist strategy in a developing economy is caused by the relatively low level of education of the population and the scarcity of experts. While foreign technology may be readily available, the inability to man the new industry with properly qualified workers and managerial staff will probably lead to a serious under-utilization of productive capacity, even though high rates of growth of output may still be achieved. On the other hand, if the government pursues a strenuous education campaign – as in Albania – the high initial levels of inefficiency should decrease quite rapidly, as appears to have been the case in Albania since 1970.

Third, the adoption of a strategy concentrating on heavy industrial development is inconsistent with a policy of self-reliance unless domestic industry is able to produce sufficient capital goods or exportables to cover the cost of the investment necessary to maintain a high rate of growth. The Albanian economy has received lavish aid for the past thirty years, and, as the discussion in the next chapter will show, the aid has definitely fostered economic growth. However, the fact that Albania was forced to slow down its rate of industrial development as recently as 1975 as a consequence of a reduction in foreign aid must raise serious doubts about the Stalinist development strategy as a vehicle for early economic independence.

Finally, the essentially macroeconomic nature of the Stalinist model should be noted. It was not until the PLA placed the strategy in a microeconomic context, based on Albania's resource endowment, that heavy industry began to show signs of a significant take-off relative to other branches. It is perhaps stressing the obvious to state the conclusion that the Stalinist development strategy is likely to yield desired economic outcomes only if, at first, priority is given to the development of those branches best served by the existing resource base.

CHAPTER 4

THE IMPACT OF FOREIGN AID ON ALBANIAN ECONOMIC DEVELOPMENT

A study of the impact of foreign aid on economic development in Albania can be based on two main questions.[1] First, how far was foreign aid indispensable to achieving the pace and pattern of economic growth desired by the PLA – as distinct from simply imports of capital goods, which were obviously essential for any significant investment in industry while Albania's own machinery-producing capacity remained negligible? Second, to what extent did the conditions of aid (and trade) acceptable to the donors and/or to Albania prove a constraint on the PLA's objectives – conditions including the 'commodity inconvertibility' of aid and, to a large extent, even of traded imports?

THE MACROECONOMICS OF AID

A basic prerequisite of economic growth is investment and thus savings. The absence of a sufficiently high level of savings to produce a desired rate of growth of output may be due either to the characteristics of the economic system or to the level of development of the economy. Thus, in a market economy investible resources may be potentially available, but decentralized decision-making may lead to relatively higher levels of current consumption than might be the case in an equally endowed centrally planned economy. On the other hand, if, regardless of the system rules that could determine the allocation of resources between investment and consumption, the economy lacks the specific resources required to generate either sufficient output of capital goods or the exports with which to pay for their import from abroad, it is clear that external sources of investment finance need to be found. The orthodox macroeconomics of aid is concerned primarily with the elucidation of models in which foreign capital is employed to meet the requirements of the developing economy by filling either of two so-called 'gaps' – viz., the savings gap (the constraint in the first case above) or the foreign exchange gap (the operative constraint in the second case).

The savings gap may be explained with reference to the Harrod growth equation:

$$g = sk$$

where g is the proportional rate of growth of national income, s is the proportion of income saved and invested, and k is the incremental output–capital ratio.

If a country receives a proportion a of national income as aid and all the aid is invested, the growth rate becomes $(a + s)k$. Assuming that k remains constant, the rate of capital accumulation necessary to achieve a target rate of growth g^* is given by:

$$c = g^*/k.$$

The savings gap is the amount of aid needed to supplement domestic savings if g^* is to be achieved, namely:

$$a = c - s.$$

If the marginal propensity to save is greater than the average ($s' > s$), then a given inflow of aid will not only increase the rate of accumulation by supplementing domestic savings, but also will raise per capita income and thus the proportion of income saved. In this case, foreign aid has increased the economy's capacity for growth, and it may be argued that eventually the target rate of growth will become 'self-sustaining'.

To turn to the foreign exchange gap – it is generally assumed that in any given time period in a developing economy there is a fixed upper limit on the value of exports, $\overline{X}$, and the requirement for imports (M) is likely to be a function of national income, mY. The foreign exchange gap is defined as the difference between imports and exports and is positive if the desired level of growth demands imports greater in total value than exports. In proportional terms:

$$a = m - \overline{X}/Y.$$

In an *ex-post* sense, of course, the foreign exchange gap must always equal the savings gap:

$$I + X \equiv S + M$$

i.e.,

$$I - S \equiv M - X$$

i.e.,

$$a = c - s \equiv m - X/Y.$$

On the other hand, the *ex ante* difference in magnitude of the two gaps will determine which is the binding constraint on growth.

Keith Griffin has argued, however, that the degree of inflexibility assumed by the two-gap model is unrealistic; that in the long run 'no economy is so rigid that it can produce neither capital goods, nor export goods nor import substitutes'.[2] Thus, he argues, it is only a government's unwillingness to switch from production for consumption to production for export that makes foreign exchange appear as the binding constraint. 'In other words, ultimately there can only be one constraint on investment, viz. savings.'

Having thus eliminated the foreign exchange gap as a long-term problem, Griffin then concentrates his attack on the savings gap formulation. He suggest that it involves two unrealistic assumptions: first, that the incremental output–capital ratio is invarient with foreign capital inflows; and, second, that foreign aid increases the level of investment by supplementing an unchanged or even increased level of domestic savings. In his view, foreign credit will tend to reduce the incremental output–capital ratio: first, the political objectives of donor countries often lead to aid being concentrated on 'large, dramatic highly visible projects which can stand as monuments to the generosity of the donors'; second, aid agencies have an ideological bias against government ownership of directly productive activities, which leads to the provision of aid that 'tends to alter the pattern of investment in favour of social overhead capital and economic infrastructure; third, for cost reasons there is a greater likelihood of large rather than small projects being aid-financed; and, finally, the provision of tied aid often results in higher import, and thus domestic production, costs for the recipient of aid.

With respect to the impact of aid on domestic savings, Griffin argues that foreign capital inflows tend to supplement consumption rather more than investment, and that the ready 'availability of debt finance [from foreign sources] on soft terms may reduce the incentive of local investors to save'; while a government in receipt of aid may consequently increase the share of public consumption in its budget.

Griffin and others have produced evidence from developing countries' experience in support of these arguments, related, as was the two-gap model, to the impact of foreign aid on developing 'mixed' or pure 'market' economies. Here, an attempt is made to test whether either of these theories appears to be supported by the effects of Soviet and Chinese aid on the Albanian economy. If either a savings gap or a foreign exchange gap exists, increased receipt of aid should have no discernible effect on the output–capital ratio, while in the Griffin case the ratio should decline with increases in aid. If domestic saving is the binding constraint, then an increase in aid would be expected to yield an increase in investment of about the same amount, or possibly slightly more. If the foreign exchange gap is the binding constraint, it is assumed that only an amount, say A of foreign aid, is required to supplement a prevailing rate of domestic savings to achieve a desired rate of growth. In other words, the additional foreign aid will allow a significant amount of potential savings that previously could not be converted into investible capital to be now so employed. Thus, if the ratio of imported to domestic investment funds is n then an increase in aid of A will lead to an increase in investment of A/n. However, since in practice no economy is ever so perfectly geared to the receipt of aid and the conversion of potential savings into investment, the amount A/n is also a maximum. In the Griffin case, any increase in aid will be met by a less than equal increase in investment, no change at all, or (less likely) a decrease.

The problem of the reliability of Albanian statistics has already been mentioned and is discussed in Appendix C below, where the background calculations to the following analysis are also given. It seems reasonable to equate the extent of foreign aid flowing into the Albanian economy with the Albanian balance of payments deficit on current account, since invisible flows both in or out of the country are likely to be very small and possibly only slightly in Albania's favour when the Soviet Union had a naval base at Vlorë.[3] Thus, the annual value of foreign aid is obtained by subtracting the value of exports from that of imports (see Table 3.4) and converting the series into constant prices for purposes of comparison with a gross investment series in 1971 prices which has been published.[4]

The Albanian industrial capital stock was estimated in the previous chapter. However, the incremental output–capital ratios used here must be calculated for the economy as a whole, as the ratio of the change in net material product over any period to gross investment in the same period (both valued in the constant prices of 1971). Two equations are then estimated for four important periods in Albania's economic development:

$$\Delta I = a\,\Delta A + b \qquad (1)$$

$$\Delta\left(\frac{\Delta Y}{I}\right) = d\,\Delta A + e \qquad (2)$$

where I is gross investment, A is foreign capital inflow, and Y is net material product.

The first period chosen is 1948–61, when Albania's main source of aid was the Soviet Union. The second is that of the Soviet presence in Albania between the first post-New Course year 1955 and the rupture of relations in 1961. The remaining two periods are those when China was the major aid donor, 1961–6 being a time of adjustment to the change in external economic relations and 1962–70 including also years when the adjustment may be supposed to have been completed.

In the case of equation (2), the results are similar for all periods, the regression coefficient never being in excess of 0.1, and although all values of d were positive, none was greater than 0.001 statistically significant. Thus, it appears that foreign aid had no perceptible impact on the incremental output–capital ratio in Albania between 1948 and 1970; and it may be noted that empirical evidence in support of Griffin's hypothesis for other developing economies is somewhat limited.[5] However, this conclusion for Albania could be rather shaky, given the evaluation of the incremental output–capital ratio as $\Delta Y/I$.[6] None the less, the result obtained accords with the assumption of the two-gap model that $\Delta Y/I\ (=k)$ does not vary with aid.

In assessing the impact of a change in aid on changes in the level of investment, the following equations were obtained:

1948–61

$$\underset{}{\Delta I} = \underset{(0.51)}{1.52\ \Delta A} + \underset{(26)}{70} \quad R^2 = 0.372 \tag{3}$$

1955–61

$$\Delta I = \underset{(0.29)}{1.82\ \Delta A} + \underset{(16)}{103} \quad R^2 = 0.865 \tag{4}$$

1962–70

$$\Delta I = \underset{(1.00)}{2.59\ \Delta A} + \underset{(50)}{67} \quad R^2 = 0.416 \tag{5}$$

1961–6

$$\Delta I_t = \underset{(1.21)}{4.19\ \Delta A_t} + \underset{(1.30)}{3.05\ \Delta Y_{It-1}} - \underset{(302)}{640} \quad R^2 = 0.710 \tag{6}$$

where $\Delta Y_{It\text{-}1}$ is the change in global industrial product lagged by one year.[7]

Equation (3) suggests that every additional \$100 of aid to Albania during the Soviet presence yielded an increase of \$152 in investment. However, if (3) is taken in conjunction with (4), it appears that the impact of aid was increased after the New Course, when absolute levels of foreign credit were reduced. Indeed, although the estimation of equation (1) for the 1948–54 period yields no statistically significant value for the relevant coefficient, the evidence of equations (3) and (4) makes it possible that it had a value close to unity during the period. The equation obtained was as follows.

1948–54

$$\Delta I = \underset{(1.04)}{0.93}\,\Delta A + \underset{(49)}{31} \quad R^2 = 0.072$$

Thus, it is not clear whether the aid that Stalin gave Albania had a positive or negative effect on domestic saving; nor may any positive conclusion be drawn on the nature of the binding constraint on the investment level. The relatively high import content of investment during the period would tend to depress the coefficient, while it is plausible that an economy as backward as Albania was at that time, with so generous a donor as the Soviet Union, could have greater difficulty in generating domestic savings than in obtaining foreign exchange. Economic decision-making power was being centralized only very slowly during this period, the larger part of national income being generated by an agricultural sector still in private ownership; and until the Albanian government was able effectively to procure the agricultural surplus, as a result of changes in planning and the increasing pace of collectivization in the late 1950s the impact of foreign aid on the Albanian economy could well have been similar to that of foreign credit on 'mixed' developing economies. However, two factors would have militated against aid producing a relaxation of the effort to generate domestic saving, as argued by Griffin. First, Soviet aid came largely in the form of plant and machinery and was not directly 'fungible'. Only if the receipt of aid had induced the Albanian government to relax its effort to squeeze out exports of 'consumables' or to use earned foreign exchange to import consumer goods could there be a 'leak' of aid to increasing consumption. Here the second factor becomes significant: the Albanian authorities' determination to concentrate resources on investment to the extent of their power to do so.

From 1955 onward, the nature of the growth constraint on the Albanian economy appears to have changed significantly, as indicated by equations (4), (5), and (6), which suggest the existence of a predominating foreign exchange gap. Although the (changing) donors remained generous and the low level of development of the Albanian economy had not changed markedly, the development of the Stalinist economic system came to ensure the high domestic savings rate demanded by the Stalinist development strategy. The different estimates of the 'impact' coefficient in (4), (5) and (6) above reflect the fact that, in the period immediately following the split with the Soviet Union, the import content of investment fell as the economy had to be adjusted from the almost exclusive utilization of Soviet and East European technology to a mixture of Comecon and Chinese production processes. It is unlikely that this adjustment period exceeded five years, and it is thus arguable that the decrease in the coefficient *a* during the late 1960s implied by equations (5) and (6) reflects the increased import content of investment that accompanied high rates of growth of investment and output during the Fourth Five-year Plan (1966–70).

The fact that the introduction of lagged industrial output into the equation for 1961–6 improves its explanatory value could be interpreted as evidence that changes in the level of investment were increasingly financed out of increases in domestic output, implying that the government decided to attempt to sustain a high note of economic growth even without recourse to any greater absolute volume of foreign assistance than had previously been available. The reduction in the import content of investment, already mentioned, supports this argument. The size of the $\Delta Y_{It\text{-}1}$ coefficient (3.05) reflects the relatively low proportion of gross industrial output in gross domestic product. Thus, for every \$100 increase in industrial output, there is implied an additional \$205 forthcoming from other sectors which could be converted into investment funds. Between 1961 and 1966 the contribution of industry to net material product in Albania averaged one-third; thus the coefficient estimated is consistent with a marginal propensity to save during the period of very nearly unity. This result indicates that the rather large standard error of the estimate (1.30) is significant. On the other hand, it is clear that the Albanian government cannot have been certain that aid to replace that from the Soviet Union would be so readily available in the future. The failure of changes in output to influence investment, indicated in equation (5), signals a return to the former dependence on foreign aid for investment in the Albanian economy in the late 1960s. The high rate of growth of industrial production during the Fourth Five-year Plan (1966–70) – 83 per cent, as against the 39 per cent growth achieved during the previous five years – was probably instrumental in convincing the Albanian authorities that reliance on generously donated aid was a more practical policy, notwithstanding the rhetoric of self-reliance, than ideologically motivated abstinence.

THEORETICAL IMPLICATIONS

The Albanian experience of foreign aid suggests that neither the two-gap model nor Griffin's alternative are entirely suitable as explanatory theories. To the extent that the Albanian economy has exhibited some evidence of both savings gap and foreign exchange gap, it may seem that the two-gap model is plausible; and such a conclusion would be reinforced by the finding that foreign aid does not appear to have affected the efficiency of capital utilization. However, the assumption of functional relationships between the major variables here considered need not hold for a centrally planned economy, since most macro-economic variables are determined far more by planners' preferences than in a market or a mixed economy. Thus, there is little reason, *a priori*, to expect gross investment to be closely correlated with either foreign aid or capital goods production, since the annual rate of invest-ment is determined centrally in the light of both economic and political considerations of importance to the planners. On the other hand, the availability of external funds, *plus* the practical possibility of squeezing domestic consumption, places an upper limit on the level of investment. The two-gap model gives a reasonable fit for the impact of aid on the Albanian economy because its two basic assumptions are fortuitously correct. First, the assumption that the rate of growth will increase if the ratio of investment to national income rises is likely to be true where ideological factors demand that ever-increasing proportions of investment funds be allocated to the production of capital goods. Second, it will generally follow that the rate of investment rises as capital imports increase if the government of a centrally planned economy is determined that it should be so and is able to ensure that domestic resources have been allocated in such a way as to facilitate the rapid absorption of the imported capital into the production process.

It was noted above that, according to Griffin, in the long run no economy is so inflexible that a foreign exchange gap need exist. The foreign exchange gap formulation argues that the economy is unable to attain a desired rate of growth because the production of exports – or import substitutes – is not sufficient to pay for or replace the required imports. It is the centralization of economic decision-making that again poses a problem in this case, since Albania's foreign exchange gap may be 'voluntary' – the Albanian government may be prepared to run a deficit in its balance of payments so long as generous aid is forth-coming. To the extent that this argument holds, the 'gap' may be illusory, and the political constraints on the choice of trading partners for a socialist economy may add to this illusion.

Griffin's theory is not appropriate for the study of centrally planned developing economies for the same reason that the two-gap model appears to provide good results: namely, the assumptions he makes concerning aid leakage to current consumption and diminishing efficiency of capital utilization are inconsistent with a Stalinist development strategy.

In the discussion thus far, the theoretical implications of donor motivation have not been considered. The two-gap model ignores the problem, assuming implicitly that economic aid has no political implications; while Griffin argues that aid agencies in the developed capitalist economies are likely to provide aid that both retards economic growth and favours the private ownership of the means of production. Centrally-planned economies such as Albania (and at an early stage North Korea),[8] seeking aid largely from other socialist economies, have certainly had no need to worry about the second of these biases, and the prevailing development strategies of both 'socialist' donors and recipients require that foreign aid directly supports economic growth above all. But sensitivity to the relationship between the nature of foreign aid and the development strategy may nevertheless have been an important factor in the split between Tirana and Moscow. The Albanian press has repeatedly accused the Soviet government of attempting to hinder the development of heavy industry in Albania, claiming that Soviet economic aid was intended primarily to make the Albanian economy a dependent part of Comecon. If the accusation is true, this does not mean that Soviet aid was ineffective in supporting Albanian economic growth; but it would be productive of tension between donor and recipient, as the Albanians felt that the aid they were receiving was not of an optimal composition, given their Stalinist development strategy. If a donor more willing to provide aid in a form more compatible with this strategy – plant and machinery for the production of capital goods – appeared on the horizon, the temptation to change to the new donor would be very strong. The change would involve economic and social costs in adapting to a new technology, and the possibility of making the change would depend on political (military and strategic) independence of the original donor. Albania could, in practice, cut its ties with the Soviet Union: Mongolia probably could not.

FOREIGN AID AND SELF-RELIANCE

It was noted above that the basic assumption of the two-gap model is that as capital imports increase the investment rate will rise and stimulate the rate of economic growth; and it has been suggested that this assumption is likely to hold true for a socialist centrally planned economy developing along Stalinist lines. To the extent that aid allows the attainment of a desired rate of growth, g^*, it is to be expected that, if the marginal propensity to save is larger than the average by more than the size of the savings gap, then the target rate of growth will eventually become 'self-sustaining'. If a foreign exchange gap is the binding constraint and the size of the savings gap is considerably less, so that increases in the amount of aid have a marked impact on investment, the growth rate g^* would become 'self-sustaining' more rapidly still. In a market developing economy with no strong political ties with the donor(s), it might be expected that, as the possibilities for self-reliance rose, the level of aid would automatically fall as a direct consequence of an increasing supply of exports or a decrease in demand for imports.

In a socialist economy various political and ideological factors are likely to complicate the situation. According to Stalinist ideology, a socialist economy must maintain a high rate of growth, and must ensure that the rate of growth of capital goods production exceeds that of consumer goods output. Consequently, the PLA leadership argued that the pattern of investment must be such as to encourage the development of heavy industry. On the other hand, as the discussion in the previous chapter showed, the Albanian economy was not able to increase the share of heavy industrial output in total industrial production until the Fourth Five-year Plan (1966–70) because a set of priorities for the development of the various branches of heavy industry had not been determined and because the larger part of Soviet aid was directed into other sectors. Thus, although it might have been possible for the Albanian economy by, say, 1965 to sustain some not-insignificant *rate* of growth without recourse to further aid, the *pattern* of growth implied by a policy of self-reliance would have run counter to the ideologically determined development strategy.

However, the problem of what an acceptable target rate of growth would be in a socialist economy remains. If it is set very high, and if it is to be even remotely compatible with 'the securing of the maximum satisfaction of the constantly rising material and cultural requirements of the whole of society' and with 'the continuous expansion and perfection of socialist production on the basis of higher techniques',[9] it is likely to require external assistance virtually throughout the process of development to a fairly high stage of industrialization. It was argued in the last chapter that the Albanian notion of self-reliance today, and for some time to come, strongly implies dependence on existing – unsatisfactory – levels of technology. Hence it is likely that a socialist economy growing from the Albanian level of development, and with the PLA's ambitions, would continue to require foreign aid at a stage when a similarly placed mixed or market economy ceased to do so.

From a political viewpoint, the continued granting of aid by a donor such as the Soviet Union may yield benefits in terms of increased influence within the socialist bloc that more than compensate for the cost of the aid. Thus, the sharp increase in aid to the Albanian economy in 1950 was probably due more to an attempt by the Soviet government to convince the PLA leadership that it had acted correctly in breaking with Yugoslavia, than to any economic motivation. But by 1956 the Soviet Union wanted to change to a 'pay-off' approach, and recommended that the Albanian economy expand fruit-growing and other agricultural sectors. It is arguable that the decision to convene the Comecon Council in Tirana in 1956 showed this shift towards getting some economic return from Albania. In the light of events that followed, it is conceivable that Hoxha did not want to give a return at all – and certainly not to develop his economy to give a return in the form apparently desired.

Political factors and the nature of the planning system may account for the receipt of higher levels of foreign aid than the donor has anticipated. Thus, in attempting to explain Albania's success in being permitted to maintain a balance of payments deficit throughout the 1950s, Wiles[10] has argued that, following the signing of trade agreements with other Comecon countries, the Albanians intentionally under-fulfilled their export plans. He cites GDR–Albanian trade statistics from Prior in support of his argument (Table 4.1).

TABLE 4.1 *GDR trade with Albania* ('000 old valuta roubles)

	GDR exports			*GDR imports*		
	Contracted	*Actual*	*Actual as % of contracted*	*Contracted*	*Actual*	*Actual as % of contracted*
1952	9,315	9,530	102	1,160	1,890	163%
1953	12,008	11,615	97	3,291	2,489	76
1954	14,179	8,622	61	3,941	2,314	59
1955	22,880	24,232	106	9,400	5,070	54
1956	15,914	16,696	105	8,074	6,612	82
1957	24,027	17,068	71	11,195	9,113	81
1958	24,668	21,969	89	18,710	10,150	54
1959	27,307	27,700	101	23,883	19,172	80

Source: F.L. Pryor, *The Communist Foreign Trade System*, London, 1963, p.192.

If Wiles's hypothesis is correct, the Soviet New Course probably accounts for the GDR's severe under-fulfillment of this part of its export plan in 1954. On the other hand, Albania's failure to meet her plans after a surprisingly auspicious beginning may also be explained by the generally ambitious nature of Albanian planning during that period, and the consequent inability of the export-producing sectors of the economy to cope with the taut planning. That this hypothesis is possibly more likely than Wiles's is suggested by the comparison in Table 4.2 between the annual percentage increase in Albanian exports to the GDR between 1952 and 1959 and the percentage rise in total exports. These two series suggest that any conclusion on the Albanian government's attempts to inflate its receipts of aid is hardly soundly based on data for trade with the GDR alone.

TABLE 4.2 *Albanian total exports and trade with GDR: annual percentage increments*

	1953	*1954*	*1955*	*1956*	*1957*	*1958*	*1959*
Exports to GDR	32	-7	119	30	38	11	89
Total exports	-16	-7	28	43	56	1	16

Source: Tables 3.4 and 4.1

Finally, it should be noted that the available evidence on Albanian investment and aid receipts does not support the conclusion that the Albanian economy had come closer to a state of self-reliance by the mid-1970s, though aid has certainly contributed substantially to economic growth. Taking the ratio of foreign aid to gross investment as a measure of the extent of Albanian self-reliance, the average values in Table 4.3 are obtained for the first five five-year plans. If the ratios did

TABLE 4.3 *Ratio of foreign aid to gross investment*

Plan period	*1951–5*	*1956–60*	*1961–5*	*1966–70*	*1971–5*
(A/I)	0.23	0.17	0.11	0.12	0.15

Source: see Appendix C.

indeed measure adequately the extent to which foreign aid had helped the Albanian economy to become self-reliant, it would even appear that aid had been detrimental since 1966; and the official Albanian claim that a major feature of Albania's development strategy is self-reliance would appear not to be borne out by these results. On the other hand, it may be that a realization of the gap between theory and practice on the part of the PLA leadership, together with dissatisfaction over the timing of Chinese deliveries in recent years, has led the Albanian government more recently to reduce its dependence on capital imports from China.

An article in *Zëri i popullit* in 1977 criticized various of the theories underlying China's foreign policy, although China was not mentioned by name. In particular, it was argued that the United States and the Soviet Union were equally dangerous superpowers and that the Third World could not be considered as a shield against their power. Later, in July, reports from Belgrade suggested that the Albanian government had asked Chinese experts to leave Albania, but official sources in both Tirana and Peking denied the reports.[11] On the other hand, the Chinese press attacked what it called 'splitism' in Albania. From the viewpoint of economic aid, a significant report broadcast by Radio Tirana on 26 July contended that the Albanian government had asked the Soviet government for credits to assist in the construction of the metallurgy complex at Elbasan in 1960 and that they had been refused. The likely validity of this contention is supported by the fact that Rumania's request to the USSR for a steel plant at Galaţi was also turned down at the same time.[12] Moreover, the Czech government had earlier said that it could supply all of Albania's steel requirements if it received Albanian ferro-nickel ores. The report went on to add that the Albanians were thus forced to build the complex relying on their own resources, and that this had been done successfully so far. That the project could not have been undertaken without Chinese aid was not mentioned; indeed, the Chinese were not thanked for aid at all. By 1978 the split between China and Albania had become total; and, since relations appear unlikely to be restored in the near future, Albania has been forced to embark on a policy of self-reliance, with all that it implies for the already low level of current consumption in the country.

If the PLA leadership decides that Albania should maintain a balance of foreign trade, it is possible that a large part of that trade will be with the developed capitalist economies of Western Europe. The agreement signed between the Albanian and Greek governments[13] to open a Tirana–Athens air link may have been a first step in this direction. However, should Albania's pattern of trade alter in this direction, now that China has lost the status, in the Albanian press, of a socialist economy, any future Albanian requirement for foreign credit would pose constitutional problems for the PLA, since article 28 of the constitution states:

> The granting of concessions to, and the creation of, foreign economic and financial companies and other institutions or ones formed jointly with bourgeois and revisionist capitalist monopolies and states, as well as obtaining credits from them, are prohibited in the People's Socialist Republic of Albania.[14]

As Kaser has pointed out, 'no government in the world has ever asked its legislature constitutionally to disbar it from raising an external loan'.[15] On the other hand, the text is fully consistent with Albania's official development strategy, and its interpretation may prove to be equally flexible.

CONCLUSION

On the basis of the discusssion throughout this chapter, it is possible to draw conclusions that relate to both the theory of economic aid and the Albanian experience. Theoretically, it might be expected that an underdeveloped economy in which a Stalinist government comes to power would display savings gap behaviour while ownership of the means of production remains private and the government has not gained control over the agricultural surplus. But as nationalization and the central planning system develop, a high rate of domestic savings, coupled with a desire to give priority to industrial development, may give the impression that a foreign exchange gap is the binding constraint. In either case, of course, the constraint may appear the more severe because the target rate of growth has been set higher than it would have been in a mixed or market economy at a similar level of development.

A study of the Albanian experience also suggests that a theory of aid that does not take account of ideological and political factors can never fully explain the impact of aid on a centrally planned developing economy; and the Albanian split with the Soviet Union provides the most dramatic illustration of this point.

It also seems reasonable to conclude that, while Albania has been able to obtain a fairly steady flow of external credit up to the mid-1970s, this aid has actually acted as a constraint on Albanian industrial policy in two important respects. First, the aid received from Comecon assisted the development of light industry in Albania rather than heavy industry, because of its commodity composition, even though it implied eventual benefits for Albanian export trade. It also operated to the detriment of agriculture up to 1953, but this appears to have been a failure of PLA policy rather than a constraint imposed by the donors. Second, the aid provided by China seems – in its composition – to have been fully in accord with a Stalinist strategy, but the problems of transport between China and Albania and China's instability as an aid donor may account for Albanian difficulties in completing the construction of industrial projects within the planned time.

CHAPTER 5

CONSUMPTION AND MOTIVATION IN THE ALBANIAN ECONOMY

In Chapter 2 it was suggested that the extent to which the Albanian economic system facilitated rapid industrial development would have been influenced significantly by the impact of the ideological campaigns on the Albanian worker. Subsequently, it has been argued that foreign aid contributed significantly to Albanian industrial development while, at the same time, acting as a constraint on the nature and speed of growth implied by the Stalinist development strategy. Similarly, it will be argued here that the measures necessary in the field of consumption to ensure the absence of significant conflict between the goals of the PLA leadership and the desiderata of individual economic agents were not entirely consistent with the consumption policy implied by the Stalinist development strategy. An analysis of the PLA's attempts to resolve this contradiction can throw light on the political prerequisites for the maintenance of a Stalinist development strategy in an underdeveloped economy. The first is that the central authorities must have almost ubiquitous political power.

CONSUMPTION AS A CONSTRAINT ON ECONOMIC GROWTH

Stalin's basic economic law of socialism requires that socialist production secure 'the maximum satisfaction of the constantly rising material and cultural requirements of the whole of society.[1] Three important policy desiderata emerge from this formulation. First, since requirements are always rising, their satisfaction implies that the real income of the population must rise annually. Stalin's dictum might thus be stated in other words: depending on the extent of domestic savings required by the development strategy, the level of current consumption in the phase immediately following the revolution may need to be depressed so that it can be seen to rise under socialism.

Second, it should be noted that Stalin is concerned with 'requirements' as distinct from 'wants'. Thus, whereas an individual is likely to be best able to define his own 'wants', because they are subjective, a Marxist-Leninist may argue that 'requirements' are objective, and will be known to the individual only if that individual's consciousness has reached the appropriate level. This argument allows the ruling party to define 'requirements' subject only to the constraint that they must be rising, and has enabled the PLA to show that fulfilment of the basic law in Albania is, by definition, inevitable:

Thus, under socialism the economic and social basis for the division of production into essential output and surplus product is eliminated. The members of a socialist society are owners of the means of production; therefore the created social product serves directly for the fulfilment of their requirements. It is divided into production for self and production for society in accordance with the general interest in development and in the uninterrupted increase in the well-being of the working masses.[2]

The use of the phrase 'working masses' leads to the third corollary of the basic law. Stalin refers to 'the whole of society', and this might be interpreted to require that either the income – suitably defined – of the population as a whole, or the income of every individual in the society, is continually rising. But the PLA has clearly interpreted the law as requiring that the real income of peasants and blue-collar workers ('the working masses') must be increasing over time. It seems reasonable to conclude that the goal as interpreted by the PLA will have been fully met if the consumption fund has grown more rapidly than the population every year and if the real income of the 'working masses' has likewise risen.

Since the Stalinist development strategy requires the highest possible rates of growth of industrial output, the necessity to increase current levels of consumption is a constraint on its execution. However, since the aim and means are dialectically linked, the economic laws should provide an upper limit to consumption as well as the lower limit already formulated. Thus, according to the Albanian formulation, the upper bound of the consumption fund is given by the desired size of the accumulation fund as a proportion of national income, while the rate of growth of industrial production of consumer goods, group B, may never exceed that of group A, the production of capital and intermediate goods.

The Stalinist development strategy, *per se*, does not indicate the way in which the consumption fund should be divided, either between social and individual consumption or between various groups in the society. On the other hand, the distribution of income will influence economic development via the labour market and material incentives. Thus, in areas of free choice, wages rates will help determine the allocation of labour. Once a given distribution of the labour force has been established, changes in absolute and relative levels of wages will be important factors in determining whether, and to what extent workers' aspirations conflict with the goals of the leadership.

In a backward economy with virtually no industrial base, the initial rate of domestic savings required by the Stalinist strategy is clearly very high. Thus if, as has already been suggested, the consumption fund must at first fall below its pre-revolution level, the distribution of the fund may have an important effect on the functioning of the system. If, before the change in government, the vast majority of the population was extremely poor, with the major part of increases in real income being allocated – administratively or via market forces – to a wealthy minority, then it may be possible, after the revolution, to decrease the consumption fund while increasing the real income of the majority of the population by a redistribution of consumable wealth from rich to poor. In this way, the legitimacy of the new rulers is enhanced and the majority is satisfied that the new system is responsible for an increase in their real income. Moreover, if the revolution has been accompanied by considerable economic loss, as for example during the Second World War, the leadership is able to appeal to nationalist sentiment in a bid to achieve a high rate of savings, and may point to war losses as being responsible for any reduction in the real income of the majority which redistribution has been unable to compensate. But difficulties begin to arise if the rate of growth of the consumption fund is not in accordance with the population's expectations. Then motivations other than material rewards and a further change in the distribution of income may become necessary if the high rate of savings is to be maintained. The Albanian experience in this area will be considered after an analysis of policy towards aggregate consumption during the first five five-year plans.

AGGREGATE CONSUMPTION POLICY, 1951–1975

The relative rates of growth of group A and group B production were discussed in Chapter 3, where it was shown that the ideological requirements were met during all but the First Five-year Plan. Table 5.1 shows the distribution of national income between accumulation and consumption during the five-year plans completed since 1951. Annual

TABLE 5.1 *Consumption as a percentage of NMP at current accounting prices*

1951–5	*1956–60*	*1961–5*	*1966–70*	*1971–5*
74.4	73.0	71.2	66.1	64.0

Source: 30 vjet Shqipëri socialiste, Tirana, 1974, p. 189.

data on the consumption fund have never been published, although an estimate based on the components of consumption is possible.

Clearly, the accumulation fund has grown more rapidly than the consumption fund in each of the five-year plan periods between 1951 and 1975. However, to gain a deeper insight into the nature of Albanian consumption policy, an estimate of annual levels of consumption must be made.

The major component of personal consumption is retail sales less purchases by institutions. Statistics for retail sales via state or co-operative outlets have been published since 1958, but the series for private sales ends in 1964. It will be assumed, on the one hand, that the ideological campaigns of the mid-1960s were responsible for a reduction in the level of non-farm private trade and, on the other hand, that the supply of agricultural products on the private market has probably increased with the growth of agricultural output. Since there are no quantitative data available on these opposite trends, it will be assumed that they have cancelled each other out and that the ratio of private to state and collective retail trade has maintained its 1964 level of 8.7 per cent.[3] Further, it will be assumed that 8.5 per cent of non-private retail trade covers purchases by institutions and that this ratio has been constant over time.[4]

The level of (non-monetized) autoconsumption of households has been reported as 30 per cent of total personal consumption in 1970.[5] It will be assumed that this variable would move parallel with changes in the output of bread grains. An unrealistic bias in the estimate would be introduced if global agricultural production were used as a surrogate for autoconsumption because the weight of cash crops in the total has increased over time. Thus, the value of autoconsumption for 1970 may be directly computed, and values for other years obtained, by weighting the 1970 estimate by an index of bread grain production. It should be noted that this estimate of autoconsumption does not take into account the production of clothing and consumer durables by rural households. However, the rapid increase in non-private retail turnover, coupled with the increasing urbanization of the Albanian population,[6] suggests that household production activities have probably been decreasing. If this is so, the calculated consumption series will tend to overstate the rate of growth of consumption and there are insufficient data available to permit correction of this bias.

On the other hand, the estimate here of social consumption will understate the increase in consumption and may offset the upward bias resulting from increasing monetization of the economy. Social consumption is calculated as the sum of annual budget expenditures on health, education and culture, social care, and social security, the provision of services such as housing, electricity, and water being excluded. No data are available on the magnitude of these latter services, although their contribution to the total is likely to be very small, given the low prices set for them by the Albanian authorities. Thus, it has been reported that the income from one or two work days is sufficient to cover rent payments while 'payment for water, electricity, and other services of the kind are symbolic'.[7] However, since these prices have probably fallen over time, not only is real consumption undervalued, but the series is biased downwards.

The final component of consumption is consumption by members of the armed forces. It will be assumed that a reasonable estimate of this is obtained by halving the annual defence expenditure in the state budget. The index of per capita consumption in Albania thus calculated is shown in Table 5.2. The series has been calculated from data at current prices, but there is evidence to suggest that it may reasonably be interpreted as a measure of the change in real consumption over time. First, the retail price indices for the 1958–64 period[8] indicate that the prices of 57 products were constant in 1963 and 1964; of 28

TABLE 5.2 *Index of per capita consumption* (1950=100)

1950	100	*1960*	184	*1966*	220	*1972*	. .
1955	145	*1961*	184	*1967*	231	*1973*	300
1956	141	*1962*	186	*1968*	242	*1974*	. .
1957	165	*1963*	188	*1969*	259	*1975*	318
1958	180	*1964*	196	*1970*	265		
1959	212	*1965*	200	*1971*	277		

Source: See Appendix C.

food goods, 3 retailed at their 1958 prices in 1964, the prices of 24 goods fell by between 4.5 and 24.25 per cent, while the price of eggs rose by about 15.5 per cent. The retail prices of 8 of the 29 non-food items remained constant over the 1958–64 period, while the remaining 21 goods maintained their price level between 1962 and 1964, their prices having fallen by between 4.5 and some 52.5 per cent between 1958 and 1962. Second, as the figures in Table 5.3 show, the prices of some commodities had already fallen by 1958 and continued to fall after 1964.

On the basis of this evidence, it might be concluded that the series in Table 5.2 understates the growth rate of per capita consumption. On the other hand, the prices of privately traded goods have probably

TABLE 5.3 *Retail prices in state shops (leks per kilogram)*

	Ration prices	*1956 (post-rationing) prices*	*1970 prices*
Bread	5.5	3.1	2.0
Flour	7.5	4.5	3.7
Rice	12.5	10.0	8.0
Sugar	18.0	13.0	8.0
Soap	13.0	10.0	6.0
Dyed calico	–	16.0	9.0
Dyed duck-cloth	–	33.6	13.7
White formed flannel	–	23.0	12.8

Source: D. Gjiriti, *Mbi mirëqenien e punonjësve të qytetit e të fshatit* (On the Well-being of Workers of Town and Country), Tirana, 1973, p. 88.

risen, owing to continuing state supply problems and the increase in agricultural costs with the continuing flow of labour into towns; and it is possible that there have been disguised price rises linked with the appearance of new goods on the market (increases in prices owing to changes in product designation are common elsewhere in Eastern Europe. That these price increases probably compensate for the increased consumption owing to price falls is suggested by the comparison between official Albanian data and those of Table 5.2, shown in Table 5.4

TABLE 5.4 *Per capita consumption – a comparison with official estimates*

	Official (1971 prices)	*Table 5.2*
1950	100	100
1960	174	184
1970	213	265

Source: Table 5.2 and Gjiriti, op.cit., p. 83.

It may be argued that the Albanian series – which measures changes in the consumption fund in real terms – is lower than the Table 5.2 estimates for two reasons: Albanian estimates of the consumption fund do not include non-material budgetary outlays – and these have increased more rapidly than personal consumption – and an increase in some prices has been taken into account in calculating the series. If this were not the case, the relatively small share of social consumption in the total and the magnitude of the price decreases cited above would lead to an official estimate in excess of that in Table 5.4. It is clear from the figures in Table 5.2 that the requirement for an annual increase in per capita consumption implied by Stalin's basic economic law has been met in most years. Further, the years of decline coincide with failures in the grain harvest, the larger part of the short fall being reflected in an assumed consequent reduction in autoconsumption; and an increase in this element explains the large rise in consumption in 1959.

Although per capita consumption has risen in most years, its rate of growth has nevertheless fluctuated markedly, as Table 5.5 indicates, largely in accordance with fluctuations in other sectors of the Albanian economy. In particular, the difficulties experienced during the Third Five-year Plan (1961–5) led to a sharp deceleration in the growth rate of consumption. On the other hand, the fact that there was any increase at all suggests that the PLA leadership attempted to maintain a close link between ideology and practice. However, it may be argued that, with elements in the PLA undoubtedly questioning the wisdom of the change in allegiance from the Soviet Union to China, to have allowed a fall in real consumption might have amounted to political suicide for the PLA leadership. As was suggested in Chapter 2, signs

TABLE 5.5 *Rate of growth of per capita consumption in five-year periods*

1951–5	*1956–60*	*1961–5*	*1966–70*	*1971–5*
45%	27%	9%	33%	20%

Source: Table 5.2.

of popular unrest in 1965 were probably instrumental in the PLA's decision to reorganize the planning system, and, while the unrest may have been due partly to the high degree of centralization of economic decision-making power, it seems more likely that it was the result of consumption levels being insufficient to satisfy the expectations of the population.

By contrast, the high rates of growth achieved during the Second and Fourth Five-year Plans attest to the rapid expansion of production; the successful fulfilment of plans in heavy industry enabled the PLA to increase the size of the consumption fund without exceeding the ideological constraint. But a failure to meet the industrial targets of the Fifth Five-year Plan produced a reduction in the rate of growth of per capita consumption in the 1971–5 period, although the growth rate of consumption was not permitted to fall as rapidly as had been the case ten years earlier.

Assuming a Stalinist development strategy in the 1951–5 period, the high increase in per capita consumption between 1950 and 1955 may at first sight appear surprising, but is less so on closer examination. While there are sufficient data to calculate the annual increments in per capita consumption, the difficulties noted by Hoxha at the end of suggest no rapid increase in the standard of living of workers or peasants up to that time. Thus, for example:

As in former years, this year, too, the population of our cities has not had the guaranteed supplies of fixed amounts of foodstuffs and industrial goods. . . .

The plans for the guaranteed supply of the urban population with many important articles have scarcely been realized in all these years. This is most apparent in such items as meat, fish, beans, eggs, rice, and cheese.[9]

Similarly, there were difficulties for the peasants, particularly the system of taxation in kind, according to which the peasant was expected to deliver a predetermined amount of produce to the state regardless of his total output.

During the years of the great drought, taxation in kind became even more burdensome for the peasant, because he did not achieve the expected yields. . . . Thus, . . . in 1946 we took from him an average of 16.9 per cent of his production in compulsory deliveries, in 1949 we took 21.6 per cent, in 1950 22 per cent, and in 1952 20.1 per cent. . . .[10]

Hoxha also reported that the available surplus for the private agricultural market had decreased significantly, falling from 221,400 quintals of grain in 1949 to 133,700 quintals in 1950 and 86,000 quintals in 1952.[11] Finally, Hoxha pointed out that 'the peasants' income from the sale of other agricultural products such as poultry, honey, pig meat, and fruit had been 'meagre'.[12] Thus a large part of the increase in per capita consumption between 1950 and 1955 very probably occurred in the two last years and was due to the change in the pattern of investments and the budgetary grants to the peasantry announced at the December 1953 Plenum of the PLA Central Committee.

It thus seems reasonable to argue bearing in mind the analysis in

Chapter 3 that the PLA has been constrained in its desire to choose high target growth rates for industry by the need continually to raise the level of current consumption, and that it has allowed increases not only for ideological reasons but also to ensure the achievement of one of its major goals: to stay in power.

THE DISTRIBUTION OF INCOME

It may reasonably be argued that a centrally planned economic system will function optimally only when all members of the system are appropriately motivated; and, at the highest level of generality and ignoring moral incentives, the greater the increase in current consumption, the narrower becomes the gap between the goals of the individual economic agents and those of the rule-makers in the system. However, this line of argument as yet ignores the spread of consumption in the economy – in other words, the distribution of income. Statistical data on the distribution of income in Albania are very scarce. However, there are sufficient published data on the PLA's conception of the ideal, and on the policy measures that have been taken to move the society towards that ideal, to allow an analysis of the motivation problem in the context of its implications for the functioning of the system and for industrialization.

For the purposes of this analysis, three income-earning groups may be distinguished: workers, peasants, and employees. A worker may be defined as any non-managerial employee of a state enterprise, industrial or agricultural. A peasant is a member of a collective farm, and an employee may be defined as any income-earner who is neither a worker nor a peasant. Thus, managers, experts, and members of the policy, planning, and administrative hierarchy are all employees. In ideological terms, workers and peasants may be said to engage in physical work, while employees perform mental work. Workers and peasants may also be distinguished in terms of their role in the dictatorship of the proletariat: 'The social essence of the dictatorship of the proletariat is the alliance between the working class and the toiling peasantry, under the leadership of the working class.'[13]

The only hint in *Economic Problems of Socialism in the USSR* relating to the distribution of income in a socialist economy is provided by Stalin's discussion of the distinctions between town and country, and between mental and physical labour.[14] Stalin argues that, under socialism, the 'antithesis' between these categories, which existed under capitalism, has been modified and has become a 'distinction'. In other words, although workers differ from managers, the latter are no longer 'enemies, but comrades and friends'.[15] Stalin expects the gap between mental and physical work to narrow as socialist emulation campaigns increase the educational level of the workers and thus make their work more 'mental' in content. Of course, under full communism, the distinction vanishes. For Stalin, the major difference between town (industry) and country (agriculture) lies in the fact that agricultural collectives are group-owned while industrial output is generated by state-owned enterprises. He provides no guidelines as to the way in which group ownership may become state ownership, though direct nationalization is ruled out. The Albanian approach to this problem is discussed in Appendix B.

It should be noted that the PLA's approach to the mental-physical work distinction has differed from the Stalinist prescription. Whereas there is agreement on the ultimate disappearance of the distinction – in the sense that under full communism all members of society will engage in physical and mental work – the PLA believes that this can be achieved only if, at earlier stages, every employee takes part in physical production work for some part of the year. This, and other 'proletarianizing' measures adopted by the PLA, have been discussed in Chapter 2, but the implications for the distribution of income of the PLA's position on these ideological matters is of interest here also.

Until the mid-1960s, pay scales were established on a basis similar to that employed elsewhere in Eastern Europe. Thus, the lack of suitably qualified experts in Albania gave rise to income differentials designed to induce people to gain higher qualifications, and remuneration was also higher for tasks that were judged to be physically difficult. In this way, not only were employees paid more highly than workers, but there was also significant spread of income between different branches. In 1960 the average worker in transport – the most highly paid sector – received 71 per cent more pay than the average worker in the food industry – the lowest paid sector.[16] No figures relating the income of workers to that of employees have been published, although it seems reasonable to assume that the ratio was probably greater than 4 to 1 (evidence to substantiate this assumption is considered below). The available statistics on changes in real income are shown in Table 5.6.

The first sign that the PLA leadership was concerned that the ratio of employee income to worker income was too high came in the PLA Central Committee's 'Open Letter' of March 1966. It is there argued that, although PLA policy had always attempted to ensure that the increase in income of any particular individual was in line with increases in the earnings of the rest of the population, there were still anomalies in various categories of the pay scale. In particular, it is pointed out that the lack of cadres had necessitated the provision of additional material incentives 'in this or that case'. In an attempt to eliminate the anomalies, and to ensure that everybody's standard of living was in

TABLE 5.6 *Index of per capita real income*

	1950	*1960*	*1965*	*1970*	*1975*
Entire population	100	159	163	191	219

Percentage increases in per capita real income over selected periods

	1951–5	*1951–8*	*1971–5*
Workers and employees	n.a.	n.a.	8.7
Peasants	25	39	20.5

Sources: Anuari statistikor i RPSh 1959, Tirana, 1959, p. 178; B. Bardhoshi and T. Kareco, *The Economic and Social Development of the People's Republic of Albania During Thirty Years of People's Power*, Tirana, 1974, p. 210; M. Shehu, *Report on the Fifth Five-year Plan,* Tirana, 1971, pp. 10, 14; *Rruga e partisë*, no. 12, 1976, pp. 11, 19.

accordance with the economic conditions of the time, it was announced that high salaries would be reduced by an unspecified amount.

The PLA's moves towards equalization of incomes initiated by the 'Open Letter' have been repeated twice in Albania since 1966. On 29 April 1967 a joint statement of the PLA Central Committee and the Council of Ministers announced that all wages over 1,200 leks a month would be reduced, while the real income of workers would rise as a result of the abolition of all forms of income tax.[17] Although the average wage of a worker in 1967 has not been published, it is unlikely to have been much less than 550 leks – the value in 1975.[18] The statement also announced that, in response to the call for 'frugality and the spirit of sacrifice' made by the October 1965 Appeal,

> the workers of our country have widely aligned themselves with the revolutionary initiatives of the editors of the 'Bashkimi' daily and have, of their own free will, expressed their willingness to renounce many supplementary and other incomes received over and above their basic salaries. Of major importance has been the initiative of the workers of some work centres in the Lurres district to turn over to the state all their state loan obligations, an initiative which has been supported by many other workers.[19]

On the other hand, the statement warned that placing moral incentives on a higher footing than material incentives did not imply 'petty bourgeois tendencies of equalization and standardization' and indicated that good work would continue to receive good pay. Payments above the basic wage were not, in fact, insignificant. Thus, in 1961 supplementary payments in one Shkodër enterprise accounted for 34 per cent of the wage fund, while in the 'Stalin' textile combine – one of the largest enterprises in the country – the corresponding figure was 22 per cent.[20] It has been stated that as a consequence of the 1967 measures the ratio of an enterprise director's salary to that of a typist was reduced to 2.5,[21] and the ratio of the average wage of workers to the highest salaries of employees was the same.[22]

The second 'instant' change in the distribution of income between workers and employees took place on 1 April 1976, when the Council of Ministers and the PLA Central Committee issued a joint Decision. The lower limit on higher salaries was reduced from 1,200 to 900 leks and all salaries above this level were to be reduced by between 4 and 25 per cent – presumably on a sliding scale. Lower and middle wages would not be affected, 'save in certain cases to preserve the necessary proportions'. The motivation for these income reductions was explained as the desire to ensure 'the further revolutionization of the cadres, bringing their standard of living nearer to the general standard of living of the masses, barring the road to career-seeking, the preference for office work, and many other evils which lead to bourgeois–revisionist degeneration.'[23]

It was also announced that writers would no longer receive payments for their publications, that there would be a reduction in the bonuses paid for scientific titles and degrees, and that the wages of state farm workers would be increased. Finally, it was decided that, henceforth, all specialists would be paid according to their area of specialization rather than the district or enterprise in which they worked.

It has been officially reported that these measures reduced the ratio of the nominal wage of an average worker to the highest-salaried employees to 1:2.[24] Although this ratio is probably the lowest in Eastern Europe – if not the world – it seems that the distribution of income between employees and workers was never severely disproportionate – if, as asserted, it was about 4:1 before 1966.

It should be noted that the PLA has also endeavoured to affect the distribution of income between town and country by regularly increasing grain procurement prices, reducing the retail price of industrial goods for agricultural use, and altering the pattern of budgetary expenditure on services in favour of the agricultural sector. This is partially reflected in the reported 20.5 per cent increase in per capita real income of the peasantry from 1971 to 1975 against the 8.7 per cent for workers and employees (see Table 5.6). A detailed discussion of these developments is beyond the scope of this book, but it seems that a large part of the increase in real income in the countryside has probably been financed out of increases in industrial labour productivity.

It seems reasonable to conclude that the increases in real income shown in Table 5.6 are the result of a series of conflicting trends. Thus, in the period prior to 1966 the policy of encouraging expertise and the general neglect of the countryside led to a distribution of income favourable to employees, though it is unlikely that the real income of any one of the three groups actually fell during these years. But since 1966 there has been a considerable change. First, there can be little doubt that the real income of employees has fallen over the period 1966–76. Second, it seems clear that the real income of peasants has grown more rapidly than that of workers and employees combined and probably faster than the real income of workers alone. Thus, in terms of the Stalinist requirements, there is no doubt that the distinctions between town and country and between physical and mental work are being reduced. However, the PLA's reasons for income redistribution have not been entirely ideological, partly because there is a fundamental contradiction between the Stalinist development strategy and the rules of the system established for its execution.

THE CONTRADICTION BETWEEN INDUSTRIALIZATION AND MOTIVATION

It has already been noted that the rapid industrialization of an underdeveloped economy requires the maintenance of low levels of aggregate current consumption. On the other hand, political and ideological factors have constrained this goal in Albania by introducing the necessity for a continued growth of consumption and real income. Moreover, it is clear that industrial goals will be met only if individual economic agents are adequately motivated, and this will be determined largely by the extent to which their material aspirations are met. These aspirations are, in turn, related both to the rate of growth of consumption and to the allocation of income between various types of consumer goods. Thus, in the early stages of development income will be spent on food, services, and simple industrial goods such as furniture, cooking utensils, and clothing. However, as the level of personal disposable income rises, demand for luxury consumer durables such as radios, televisions, washing machines, and refrigerators will be generated. E. E. Anderson[25] has called these two stages, respectively, the support stage and the sufficiency stage. According to Anderson, after a period of high forced savings in each of the East European economies the economy passes into its sufficiency stage,

as its political leadership becomes increasingly satisfied with the progress of industrialization and as they are exposed to greater pressures from the population to fulfil their promises of higher living standards. This transition is marked by an adjustment in the product mix of industry away from the production of capital towards the production of larger quantities of consumer goods, by greater emphasis on distribution and trade, and by the allocation of larger quantities of personal income to the population.

This change in policy implies a reappraisal of the Stalinist development strategy; but in the Albanian economy no such re-evaluation has taken place. The changes that have occurred elsewhere in Eastern Europe have been noted by the PLA leadership and condemned as 'revisionism'. On the other hand, the PLA leadership was undoubtedly becoming aware that a growth of personal incomes, which would lead to pressure on the industrialization drive, was, *ceteris paribus*, inevitable in Albania also. But the crucial variable was not aggregate disposable income but the distribution of income; since, given the continuing generally low standard of living, the pressure on government policy could come only from the wealthiest group in the society – the employees.

In the event, the relative, and even absolute, reduction in the real incomes of employees necessary to overcome this contradiction could be justified on ideological grounds. This would allow the government easily to silence any criticism and, possibly, even to increase its popularity with the workers, who could see that under a dictatorship of the proletariat no other group could sustain an increase in its standard of living that was greater than that of the proletariat. On the other hand, the employees would be forced to accept the reduction in real income for the same reason that they had to agree to participate in physical work and to be subjected to workers' control: failure to adjust uncritically to the new situation would almost certainly result in a reclassification from employee to worker or peasant status, with the implied further reduction in real income.

While it is not possible to test directly the hypothesis that the PLA leadership reduced employee incomes in an attempt to forestall the problems in the area of consumption that beset other Eastern European economies, there is at least evidence to suggest that undesired pressure on the consumer goods industries has been avoided. However, personal savings indicate the existence of disposable income that exceeds necessary expenditure on the bundle of goods currently being offered.

Personal savings deposits are a reasonable surrogate for total personal savings, even though a considerable proportion of personal savings is probably held in the form of cash hoards. The transition from the 'support' to the 'sufficiency' stage of development is indicated by an increase in the ratio of savings to total cash income. This latter variable is not known for Albania, but it will be assumed that the sum of total retail turnover (state, co-operative, and private) less sales to institutions, *plus* the annual change in personal savings deposits, provides a reasonable estimate of current cash income. The exclusion of cash hoarding from the calculations will probably lead to an understatement of the savings–income ratio but is unlikely to affect its trend over time. Table 5.7 shows current income and current personal savings deposits and the ratio of the two, for Albania and Hungary – the latter case having been used by Anderson in the formulation of his arguments. The greater value of the savings–income ratio at all periods for Hungary indicates the obvious fact that the standard of living is considerably higher in Hungary than in Albania. In other words, when the Hungarian population has allocated a proportion of its disposable income to achieve a desired level of consumption (of the goods and services actually available), the surplus income remaining that may be saved is greater than in Albania. The difference in the magnitude of the ratio probably understates the difference in standard of living, since the 'desired level of consumption' is unlikely to be as high in Albania as in Hungary.

The rate of growth of the savings–income ratio was considerably higher in the Hungarian economy between 1960 and 1970 than in Albania – respectively, 288 and 45 per cent; and this discrepancy reflects the differences in consumption policy in the two economies. On the basis of the rapid growth in Hungarian savings, Anderson concludes: 'the high savings rates of the population indeed imply that actual consumer demand was frequently less than that expected by central planners because households possessed and employed the discretionary power to reduce the magnitude of consumption expenditures.' This, he argues, led to an unanticipated build-up of stocks of consumer goods, which acted as a lever on the central planners to improve the output mix,[26] though the slight drop in the savings–income ratio in 1967 is probably due to a change in the relationship between savings and cash hoardings rather than to change in government policy. In Albania, however, the PLA's income distribution policy is clearly reflected in the savings–income ratio. When it is considered that the Albanian population has always been encouraged to save, the 9 per cent drop between 1966 and 1967 – the savings data are taken at the end of the calendar year[27] – is significant. That the level of accumulated personal savings was reduced in 1967, when the number of bank accounts actually rose by 23 per cent,[28] suggests that there had been a redistribution of income which impelled some members of the society to run down cash balances in order to maintain existing levels of consumption. It could also be argued, however, that

TABLE 5.7 *Money incomes and savings*

	1960	*1961*	*1962*	*1963*	*1964*	*1965*	*1966*	*1967*	*1968*	*1969*	*1970*	*1973*
(1) Personal savings deposits (million leks)	119	122	133	149	167	196	221	212	231	255	295	427
(2) Personal disposable income (million leks)	2,334	2,327	2,379	2,548	2,694	2,793	3,016	3,181	3,490	3,846	3,929	5,014
Average value of savings account (leks)	505	489	489	502	534	600	670	524	517	533	572	619
(1)/(2): Albania	0.051	0.052	0.056	0.058	0.062	0.074	0.073	0.067	0.066	0.066	0.075	0.085
Hungary	0.067	0.078	0.097	0.127	0.161	0.190	0.200	0.199	0.216	0.238	0.260	–

Sources: see Appendix C for Albanian sources. Hungarian data cited from E.E. Anderson, 'The Growth of Income, Consumer Discretion, and the Accumulation of Stocks in Socialist Economies', *Papers in East European Economics*, no. 45. Centre for Soviet and East European Studies, St Anthony's College, Oxford (mimeographed).

at a time of mounting ideological campaigns it was considered safer to transfer bank savings into cash hoards, and the real explanation of the fall in bank balances is probably a combination of both factors.

The PLA's continuous, and apparently successful, propaganda for an increase in personal savings complicates the interpretation of the growth in the Albanian savings–income ratio since 1968 in terms of discretionary income. For, while the number of bank accounts continued to rise up to 1973, the average value of an account in 1973 was still considerably lower than it had been in 1966, suggesting that the number of accounts containing large sums had fallen, with a concomitant reduction in the pressure on the supply of consumer durables; and it is likely that the redistribution measures of 1976 represented a further attempt to forestall any possible pressure.

Further evidence of the Albanian government's awareness of the dangers of inflationary pressure in a planned economy is provided by the following official criteria for the determination of output and income levels.[29]

(1) Social product, net material product, and the socialist accumulation fund must all grow more rapidly than the level of personal disposable incomes.

(2) The wage funds for workers and employees must be planned in accordance with the requirements of the 'law' that labour productivity must always grow more rapidly than average wages.

(3) The rate of growth of agricultural cooperatives' net income must exceed that of the wage fund, priority being accorded to the accumulation fund over the consumption fund.

(4) The rate of growth of production of wage-goods must exceed the rate of growth of cash in circulation.

(5) The provision of communal services must outstrip the increase in the population.

It seems reasonable to conclude that the PLA leadership has been successful in reconciling the increased material aspirations of earners of relatively high incomes with the requirements of the Stalinist development strategy. On the other hand, the increases in per capita savings balances after 1968 suggest that *ad hoc* salary cuts may continue to be necessary in the future. Further, although it is unlikely that official documents would directly reflect dissatisfaction among employees – and no unofficial evidence is available – the severe constraints placed on management by the PLA-led worker control schemes has probably guarded against serious malfunctioning of the system as a consequence of employee dissatisfaction. The employee's income advantage may however already have reached that low margin at which a further deterioration will result in mass protest, or at least in unwillingness to accept responsibility.

WORKER MOTIVATION AND THE PLANNING SYSTEM

While the PLA's income distribution policy appears to have risked inadequate motivation of employees, and specifically of enterprise management, there has also been a problem of worker motivation and labour productivity.

In terms of production function analysis, one is concerned with the distinction between a movement along the production function – where growth of output is the result of increases in the quantities of labour and capital employed in the production process – and a shift in the function, representing 'disembodied technical progress' (or regress). While there are insufficient statistical data available to estimate a reasonably accurate production function for the Albanian economy, the available evidence does permit a qualitative approach to the question. Thus, the estimates of the Albanian industrial capital stock made in Chapter 4 allow some inferences to be drawn – via changes in the industrial output–capital ratio – about the impact of the sales of the system on this kind of technical progress. Table 5.8 shows the percentage increase or decrease in the output–capital ratio over various periods since 1950.

TABLE 5.8 *Output–capital ratio: percentage changes over given periods*

	1951–5	*1956–60*	*1961–3*	*1964–70*	*1971–3*	*1974–5*
Change in industrial output–capital ratio	-29	-1	-9	-11	2	-5

Source: Tables 3.1 and 3.2

In a Harrod–Domar economy with surplus labour, any increase in labour productivity will be accompanied by an increase of equal size in the capital–labour ratio. In the real world this is rarely the case; changes in capital productivity are caused by a variety of factors, including the 'accomodation' of new capital as workers and managers became more skilled and adapted to using it, bottlenecks in the supply of raw materials, changing levels of education of the work-force, and worker motivation. While it is not possible to isolate these factors precisely, the role of worker motivation may be implied. The economic problems encountered by the PLA during the First Five-year Plan have already been considered. While a drop in capital productivity, owing to the inexperience of the workforce in coping with new equipment, could be expected during this period, this reason alone seems insufficient to explain the magnitude of the decrease compared with later periods when growth was still largely extensive. Further, given the relatively decentralized nature of the planning system, it seems unlikely that supply problems were greater than in any later period. Therefore, it seems reasonable to argue that the drop in capital productivity was probably due as much to the motivation problems resulting from material deprivation during 1951–3 as to any other factors. This hypothesis is supported by the relative stability in the output–capital ratio during the Second Five-year Plan (1956–60), when the system was becoming more centralized and the rate of new technology inflow was still high but per capita consumption was rising steadily. It may well be that the motivational impact of a steady increase in consumption, such as the 27 per cent apparently achieved during 1956–60, is likely to be stronger than an erratic, though greater, increase such as the 45 per cent registered during the First Five-year Plan (see Table 5.2), particularly since the level of consumption, as well as the rate of change, may be significant at relatively low levels.

It has already been argued that the fall in labour productivity during the Third Five-year Plan was due to a large increase in the industrial labour supply brought about by the PLA's attempts to fulfil its industrial plans at almost any cost. There were extensive appeals to national feeling from the PLA during this period, and exhortations to make cost savings wherever possible; and these and the increases in current consumption may have operated in favour of capital productivity, even though this fell somewhat.

In Chapter 2 it was argued that the decentralization in economic decision-making power within the policy, planning, and administrative hierarchy implied by the 1965 and 1966 changes of system rules would probably militate against increased allocative efficiency. This is reflected in the decrease of 11 per cent in capital productivity during 1964–70, but decentralization was possibly a less important factor than the gigantic inflow of Chinese capital during the period and the inability of the workforce to cope efficiently with the proliferation of new plant. On the other hand, capital productivity actually rose in 1971–3 while a high rate of economic growth was maintained. In Chapter 3 it was suggested that this was due partly to the increased educational level of the workers, but an examination of the motivational aspects of the changes in the system in 1966 and 1970 suggests that this accommodation of new capital was not the only important variable.

On 27 December 1969 the Ninth Plenum of the Central Committee of the PLA issued a decision 'On the Work of the Organizations of the Party and of the Masses, of the Economic and State Organs to Further Increase Productivity and Enforce Proletarian Discipline at Work'. In prefacing its decision the Central Committee admitted that the ideological campaigns had had very little impact on the Albanian workers,

> in analysing the indices of the socialist organization of work, it turns out that, in many cases, there are shortcomings and discrepancies springing from a superficial political and theoretical understanding and inadequate organization of work; from a one-sided treatment of these problems failing to bring them home to the people, their fulfilment of the average work productivity in certain branches has slowed down, as has the rate of production in general. Nor has enough work been done in explaining the orientations and directives of the party regarding the socialist organization of work, in acquainting the broad masses of workers with the objective economic laws governing them, as well as with the consequences resulting from their correct or incorrect application.[30]

The blame for this situation was levelled at the party and state organs at local level. It is clear that the incentives offered workers had been insufficient – or of the wrong kind – to induce them to act as watch-dogs for the PLA; and this is perhaps not surprising, since the law on the special enterprise fund gives administrative organs the right to determine whether an enterprise has met the requirements for the receipt of bonuses. It was noted in Chapter 3 that the law on the distribution of bonuses gives equal weight to the fulfilment of production, cost reduction, and profit plans, but the global production plan apparently retained first priority with the administrators. Further, even if bonuses has been determined according to the law, the emphasis on plan fulfilment of any sort would ensure that workers reacted in the same way as managers had previously done. An attempt would always be made to be granted the easiest plan possible, and then to over–fulfil it by a sufficiently small margin to prevent the imposition, from above, of a difficult plan in the next period. Indeed, it is difficult to envisage any material incentive scheme that would encourage workers to put pressure on management if that pressure was going to lead to a reduction in leisure time without a compensating increase in wages. But the moral incentives of the ideological campaigns also failed, and it is not unreasonable to conclude that, during the Fourth Five-year Plan, capital productivity fell partly as a result of worker dissatisfaction with the PLA's continued efforts to firmly entrench Marxism–Leninism on the shop floor.

In the light of the above arguments, the slight upswing in capital productivity during the Fifth Five-year Plan – particularly in the period 1971–3 – might be thought to be partly attributable to some change in motivation brought about by the new system rules of 1970. However, the evidence cited in Chapter 3 shows that the problems of labour absenteeism have persisted beyond 1970; and, in fact, the only change in system rules likely to contribute to an increase in workers' active support for PLA policy was the announced establishment of a special fund to be used to implement workers' innovatory suggestions. It seems more reasonable to argue that it was the re-imposition of bank control over investments and the tighter administrative control made possible by the reduction in the number of plan indicators under the new system that facilitated an increase in the efficiency of use of capital.

On balance, it is difficult to determine whether PLA policy on the motivation of workers has had a positive or negative impact on the industrialization drive. Whereas the insistence upon continually increasing the worker's standard of living has probably contributed to popular support for the regime and its goals, it appears that PLA efforts to inculcate the population with its political doctrines may have had little, or even a negative, effect on labour productivity. On the other hand, political socialization is a long-term process, and there is insufficient evidence available as yet to conclude that the PLA will not eventually be successful in this direction.

CONCLUSION

The requirements of Stalin's basic economic law of socialism with respect to consumption policy led eventually to an increase in the real income of a certain part of the Albanian population – the employees – which threatened to place pressure on the industrialization drive by increasing the demand for consumer durables beyond the limits considered appropriate by the PLA leadership. They responded with a severe reduction in the real income of Albanian cadres and the institution of a series of ideological campaigns intended to provide justification for this redistribution of income and to contribute to the motivation of Albanian workers – campaigns that had doubtful success in the latter respect.

Perhaps the most important conclusion arising from the PLA's consumption and motivation policies is of a political nature, and fairly obvious – that the enforcement of a high savings rate in a poor country and, occasionally, of a severe redistribution of income, is possible only if the central authorities have sufficient political power – in addition to economic power – to withstand popular opposition to their policies. Even in a one-party state, if this power is lacking popular unrest may lead to changes in the ruling elite with a concomitant change in development strategy. This argument is supported by the experience of several Eastern European economies in the mid-1950s, by the rise to power of Dubcek in Czechoslavakia and the events of 1970 in Poland. In the Albanian case it seems reasonable to argue that the progenitor of Albania's development strategy, Enver Hoxha, has been able to maintain his policies over the previous thirty years with relatively few modifications by striking a successful balance between the need to maintain popular support by allowing a continual increase in the standard of living of workers and peasants, and the inevitable alienation of large numbers of state functionaries and enterprise managers and experts resulting from occasional decreases in their real income. The PLA's cadre circulation policy, discussed in Chapter 2, may also have been designed to keep political power firmly in the hands of the party leadership by preventing potential opponents from creating or maintaining a stable power base.

CHAPTER 6

FINALE

It is consistent with PLA policy since 1945, as revealed in actions and ideology, to interpret the Albanian economic experience as a two-gap model of development constrained by Stalinist rules; these rules include the establishment of a centrally planned economic system and the maintenance of the maximum feasible rate of saving while ensuring a positive increment year by year in the level of current consumption. This interpretation does not ignore the influence of the contemporary Chinese leadership on Albanian policy. But whereas the Chinese impact on the PLA's foreign economic policy since 1960 has been considerable and the economic implications of Chinese aid for the direction and pace of Albania's industrialization have been far-reaching, there is almost no evidence to support the common assumption that the PLA leadership is Maoist. This erroneous assertion appears to have been based solely on the fact that China has been Albania's only staunch ally since 1961 and that Albania has deferentially used Chinese-style terminology from the time of the Cultural Revolution onwards, though it may be noted that changes in the rules of the economic system and the ideological campaigns, which began in the mid-1960s in Albania, have never been described in Albanian sources as a 'cultural revolution'.

This chapter summarizes the history of the implementation of Albania's development strategy and the evolution of the postwar economic system up to the mid-1970s.

THE ORIGINS OF ALBANIA'S DEVELOPMENT STRATEGY

The Italian presence in Albania prior to the Second World War had several important effects on the PLA leadership's approach to economic policy. On the one hand, extensive geological exploration revealed the existence of a substantial mineral resource base which could, under the appropriate circumstances, be utilized to Albania's advantage by the provision of exportables and of the energy required by new industries. It also became clear that the postwar Albanian authorities would have to find an ally willing to finance capital formation and capital goods imports to bridge the economy's savings and foreign exchange gaps. The government (somewhat accidentally) isolated itself from the United Kingdom, and hence from the West in general, by the Corfu Channel incident, and thus could not turn to the West, like Yugoslavia, in 1948. Finally, the Albanian experience with Italy led to the realization that economic penetration gave rise to political dominance, and the Hoxha regime's nationalization of non-farm assets ensured that economic aid would have to be obtained on a government-to-government basis.

Enver Hoxha's violent opposition to Koçi Xoxe and others who advocated union with Yugoslavia might be partly explained by Albania's prewar misfortune. In the event, Hoxha's victory over the pro-Yugoslav faction in 1948 probably would not have been possible without the intervention of Stalin, and gratitude may account, in part, for the PLA's uninterrupted adulation of the Soviet leader from that time onwards. The political preconditions for the adoption of a Stalinist development strategy thus existed; in terms of material resources, the extensive mineral base spoke in favour of the development of heavy industry though the lack of skilled human resources militated against it.

On the basis of the discussion in Chapters 2, 3, and 4 it seems reasonable to conclude that the PLA leadership worked to bring about a transformation of the Albanian economy such that heavy industrial development might become feasible. They faced two linked but separate problems: the achievement of high rates of economic growth, and the determination of the pattern of growth. Given the Soviet Union's generosity as an aid donor to Albania (partly to ensure continued use of a submarine base on the Adriatic), an economy as backward as was Albania at the time might have been expected to have had greater difficulty in generating domestic savings than in securing foreign exchange. However, a high rate of domestic savings would become possible only if the government were able to control the agricultural surplus, a condition that was not met until the pace of collectivization increased in the late 1950s. To this extent it may be argued that the PLA used foreign aid as a substitute for domestic savings in the generation of investment during its early years in power.

Economic assistance from the Soviet Union and other Comecon countries was also used directly to obtain the capital equipment needed for a programme of industrialization, though the possible rate of development was still severely constrained by a shortage of skilled labour. This constraint operated in two areas of the economy. Within the new industries, recently urbanized peasants were expected to man what was, to them, sophisticated equipment; and this has been an ongoing problem for the economy, though there are signs that by the beginning of the 1970s the PLA's strenuous education campaign had contributed to capital-augmenting technical progress.

In the sphere of economic management also, the Albanian government's desire to establish a highly centralized system of decision-making was hindered by a lack of suitably qualified cadres. Consequently it proved necessary to centralize the economy in a series of gradual steps, and this partly explains why the classic Soviet model of plan indicators was not in operation until 1959. But while there seems no reason to attach any other particular significance to the date when the centralized system was introduced, the considerable delay in bringing it into being may also be explained by the PLAs desire to consolidate its power base.

In relation to the pattern of Albanian economic development, relations with Comecon were not yielding, in the 1950s, the benefits for which the PLA had hoped. Thus, while aid was lavish throughout the 1950s, the kind of plant and equipment flowing into Albania from Eastern Europe was designed primarily to integrate the economy into Comecon by fostering the rapid growth of consumer goods (including food) industries. This was particularly the case after the 1955 change in Comecon policy towards the consumer goods industries, which were accorded a priority under the 'New Course' that only steel-making and engineering had enjoyed under Stalin. Under these circumstances, the Stalinist strategy of heavy industrialization could have commenced only when light industry and primary commodities provided sufficient exportables to finance the import of heavy industrial capital. The extent to which the PLA's dissatisfaction with the nature of Comecon aid influenced its reaction to the Sino-Soviet split is unclear, but there can be no doubt that the decision to forgo abundant Soviet assistance and to rely on promised aid from China – a country itself still developing – reflected a degree of ideological commitment unknown elsewhere in Eastern Europe.

Finally, the death of Stalin in 1953 and the Malenkov–Khrushchev reassessment of, *inter alia*, Stalin's agricultural policy was probably influential in encouraging the PLA leadership to re-evaluate its own farm policy. Albanian peasants had been taxed heavily while the state had undertaken insufficient investment in agriculture to provide a growing surplus in face of the increasing urbanization of the population. But the First Five-year Plan had called for self-sufficiency in food grains – a target not reached until 1976 – indicating the PLA's awareness that a rapid rate of industrial growth would be possible only if the agricultural sector were able to supply the country's food requirements, thus permitting a greater import of capital goods. The PLA leadership decided, in December 1953, to divert resources into agriculture, and to reduce the level of forced savings by that sector, so as to stimulate agricultural production. Although the PLA's emphasis had again shifted away from agriculture by the end of the Second Five-year Plan (1956–60), farm price policies have ensured increasing levels of consumption in the countryside up to the present time, and have been supplemented by the capital subsidies made necessary by the fact that the Albanian agricultural sector is still the most backward in Europe.

The economic cost of changing allies was high. Projects, the construction of which had been commenced with the aid of Soviet experts, were left incomplete, while existing plants were often without necessary spare parts. In an attempt to meet the industrial output target of the Third Five-year Plan (1961–5), human and material resources were diverted from other sectors into industry, resulting in a failure to fulfil most of the plan targets. The PLA leadership must have been aware of the possibility that the Albanian economy would require technological restructuring in the event of a break with the Soviet Union, and it seems reasonable to argue that the authorities considered that the benefits implied by independence in decision-making and the implementation of a programme of heavy industrialization would outweigh the costs of one failed five-year plan.

The necessary conditions for Stalinist development were established in Albania in 1966, when the growth rate of industrial producer goods output began to accelerate; and thereafter, there was no change in the development strategy, in terms of Stalinist ideology, until 1973, when a reduction in Chinese aid necessitated a reappraisal of priorities. While this point is considered in greater detail below, it may be noted that, whereas the fundamental tenets of Stalinist economic ideology have never been questioned in the Albanian literature, there has been a series of important changes in system and policy variables since 1965. These represent the adaptation of a development strategy, originally designed for the Soviet Union, for application by a small underdeveloped economy which must rely on foreign economic relations for achieving a high rate of growth.

THE ALBANIAN ECONOMIC SYSTEM

In the classic Soviet model economic decision-making power is highly centralized. Thus, the party leadership undertakes the generation of policy while the government administration is responsible for its execution. However, Stalinist ideological rules do not require any specific distribution of decision-making power within the policy, planning, and administrative hierarchy. In other words, a restructuring of the planning system that shifted enterprises from ministerial to regional–state–organ subordination – a noticeable trend in Albania since 1965 – could be undertaken without a revision of the ideology. So long as the state enterprise remains the recipient of plans over which it has no control and which are legally binding on it, the law of value does not determine plan targets and the Stalinist condition holds.

Further, there is no theoretical prohibition against a decentralization of economic decision-making power from the government leadership to ministeries or regional organs of the state administration. *A priori*, it might be expected that such a reorganization would lead to increased efficiency via improved information flows. However, changes in the system initiated in 1965 probably militated against increased efficiency, because the country had insufficient cadres spread throughout the economy competent to manage their new responsibilities and because the purely economic changes were accompanied by a series of ideologically motivated measures the execution of which would have to be traded off against the achievement of economic goals.

However, it seems unlikely that the Albanian reforms – if such they may be called – of 1966 and 1970 were introduced for economic reasons. Rather, it appears that the PLA leadership was concerned about its popularity, following the difficulties of the Third Five-year Plan, and decided that it would attempt to secure its power base among the two largest groups in the country: the workers and peasants. For these classes there was the promise of increased participation in the planning process and some political control over the activities of enterprise management in the field of plan execution.

It may be stressed that the PLA leadership probably expected, nevertheless, that the system and policy changes would yield benefits beyond mass support for the regime. Particularly, it could be argued that an economic system in which enterprise directors are faced with plan-tautening pressures from above – the hierarchy – and from below – worker control – would produce more ambitious plans and partly eliminate the negative phenomenon of 'hidden reserves'. However, Albanian worker participation probably merely shifted the attempts to obtain a slack plan from the director to the workers. Further, while the imposition of worker control appears to have imposed additional constraints on management, the ideological campaigns resulted in a *de facto* transfer of decision-making from Executive Committees of People's Councils to enterprise directors; and this potential re-entry of the law of value was facilitated by the elimination of bank control over the allocation of investment funds, until this change was – quite soon – reversed.

It seems reasonable to conclude that Albanian economic growth could have been faster had the system not been decentralized and the ideological campaigns not been introduced; but the relevance of such a conclusion for the Albanian case is questionable since, true to its stated aims, the PLA leadership seems to have made the indoctrination of the population with Marxist–Leninist–Stalinist principles a *sine qua non* of economic development. Indeed, a study of the Albanian approach to problems of development suggests an underlying depth of ideological conviction on the part of the PLA leadership. This is also exemplified in Appendix B below, where the formation of higher-type cooperatives in Albanian agriculture from 1971 onwards is discussed. Thus, whereas a state farm owns its machinery and the average cooperative is one of several being serviced by a machine and tractor station (MTS), each higher-type cooperative has the exclusive services of an MTS. Stalin, in his *Economic Problems of Socialism in the USSR*, had opposed the proposal by Venzher and Sanina that MTS equipment be sold to collective farms, and the Albanian authorities – unlike Stalin's successors in the USSR – have respected this. However, in terms of availability of equipment to the higher-type cooperative, there has been a *de facto* transfer of control while remaining within the Stalinist framework.

It is not possible to draw a firm conclusion about the success or failure of the ideological campaigns; but several points may be made. To the extent that workers seem aware of the PLA's political motivation, a first stage in the education process has succeeded. But the apparent existence of slack plans in the face of official exhortations for greater effort and sacrifice indicates that the population may not yet have been convinced by what it has learnt. With respect to employees, the situation is even more difficult to evaluate. Employees have faced a considerable reduction in real income and status relative to workers and peasants since 1966; but there is insufficient evidence to allow an assessment of the economic cost of potential managerial dissatisfaction.

On the other hand, the discussion of income redistribution in Chapter 5 allows certain conclusions to be drawn regarding the PLA's attempts to solve, in a unique manner, a problem that has beset all East European planned economies. This problem is that, whereas the priority given to a high rate of capital formation requires a high level of saving, both political and ideological considerations have necessitated a fairly steady increase in per capita consumption throughout Eastern Europe. Given initial differences in the distribution of wealth and a subsequent expansion of the gap by the implementation of wage policies designed to encourage, *inter alia*, personal investment in education, acquisition of skill, and acceptance of responsibility, a point was reached – in most of the economies by the early 1960s and in Albania somewhat later – when high-income groups began to demand a wider range of consumer goods than had previously been made available. Whereas the most common solution to this problem was a reallocation of resources into the consumer goods industries, ideological considerations led the PLA leadership to adopt a different approach. According to Stalinist ideology, the rate of growth of producer goods production must exceed that of consumer goods output, while the real income of the population must always be rising. Evoking the existence of the dictatorship of the proletariat in Albania and arguing for the need to reduce the differences between mental and physical labour and town and country, the PLA reinterpreted Stalin's basic law of socialism as requiring a continual increase in the real income of the 'toiling masses', thereby legitimizing a relative, or even absolute, reduction in the real incomes of employees.

In an economic sense, the trend towards egalitarianism in Albania since 1966 may be explained in terms of the principles underlying the Stalinist development strategy. In an economic system where resources are not allocated according to the laws of supply and demand it is likely that imbalance will result between the pattern of goods and services offered for consumption and that of effective demand. In the familiar macroeconomic presentation, an attempt may be made to ensure that the total supply of consumer command over goods and services is no greater than the available amount of consumer goods and services valued at current retail prices; but this principle does not resolve the problem of microeconomic equilibrium. The wider the range of goods demanded and the greater the differences between the commodity baskets sought by various groups of the population, the more difficult it becomes to achieve equilibrium in the absence of consumer sovereignty. But if it were possible for the authorities to manipulate the demand of the population so that all groups demanded a homogeneous bundle of goods, then it would but remain to provide that bundle to establish equilibrium. So if a heavy industrilization strategy is not to be placed in jeopardy, this bundle must have two features. First, it must be suffiicently small to allow the high rate of capital accumulation demanded by the authorities, yet it must also be large enough – and continually growing – to prevent costly popular unrest. Second, the bundle ideally should be composed of commodities the production of which is labour-intensive and does not compete for scarce inputs, and particularly imported inputs, which would normally be used in the capital goods-producing sectors. Foodstuffs are thus preferable to non-food goods while, among the latter, traditional household implements are more suitable than sophisticated electrical durables.

A backward agrarian economy is likely to be able to supply the growing needs of the (poor) majority of the population. However, as industrialization proceeds, the creation of a new urban elite and increased monetization of the economy leads to divergence in consumption patterns. As is suggested in Chapter 5, the PLA leadership appears to have attempted to limit this process by striving for greater equility in income distribution. In effect, the savings made by reducing employee salaries could be used to increase the level of investment in heavy industry. One problem, however, remains. Equalization of incomes requires the 'subsidization' of agricultural earnings if the norm is taken as the wage of a blue-collar worker, and this represents a leakage from potential savings. Thus, in this respect the authorities have shown themselves to be willing to trade off growth for increased current consumption – which may be seen either as a further example of the action of ideology as a constraint on growth, or possibly as a modification of the priority of growth necessary if the peasants were to be motivated to increase output fast enough to meet the increased demand for food of the growing urban population.

The impact of political considerations on economic development is also reflected in the relationship established by the Albanian authorities between capital imports and investment. It was argued in Chapter 4 that the Albanian economy displayed 'savings-gap' behaviour in the pre-1954 period, owing to the inability of the PLA to obtain control of the agricultural surplus. But during the years 1954–70 foreign exchange availability apparently became the binding constraint on investment. However, the assumptions underlying the two-gap theory of development are such that econometric estimations such as those given in Chapter 4 will appear to reflect close correspondence between the theory and reality, while crucial differences can be obscured. In Albania the rate of growth is likely to increase as the ratio of investment to national income rises, since an apparent embrace of the Feldman model demands that the rate of growth of investment funds allocated to the production of capital goods be greater than the corresponding rate for consumer goods production and that – again for ideological reasons – the central planners will attempt to ensure that domestic resources are allocated in such a way as to facilitate the rapid absorption of capital imports into the production process, with a concomitant positive correlation between imported capital and investment. But it is nevertheless misleading to explain the impact of foreign aid on the Albanian economy with reference to the conventional two-gap model. According to the theory, the existence of a foreign exchange gap implies that the economy is unable to attain a desired rate of growth because the production of exports – or import substitutes – is not sufficiently high to pay for – or replace – the required imports. Given the increase in the rate of adjustment generated by the availability of foreign aid, it is argued that at some point in the future the target rate of growth will become 'self-sustaining'. However, the Albanian experience indicates that, as long as aid is forthcoming, the authorities will raise the target rate of growth, in accordance with the demands of Stalin's basic economic law of socialism, thus maintaining a balance of payments deficit as long as it is politically feasible to do so.

Yet according to the official Albanian description of the country's development strategy, 'self-reliance' is one of the strategy's major goals; so it seems that the Albanian concept of self-reliance must be interpreted with care. Thus, whereas the emphasis placed on the generation of hydroelectric power as a priority sector since 1967 has enabled the country to become first self-sufficient and then a net exporter of energy, the attempt to increase technical efficiency and levels of output in the engineering industry by limiting the under-utilization of capital rather than by embarking on an investment programme to install new types of capital goods implies heavy reliance on existing levels of technology; and this reliance is strengthened by the policy of attempting to become self-sufficient in spare parts. Given the relatively unsophisticated nature of Albanian industry, the authorities' insistence that world advances in technology be incorporated into the production process – without replacing existing plant and equipment with new imported capital goods – seems unrealistic.

On the other hand, the emphasis on spare parts production may assist the economy in overcoming an important source of production bottlenecks in other developing economies: if an economy relies on foreign sources for intermediate goods such as small capital good replacements, key components and semi-manufactures, inability to obtain those imports – for whatever reason – is likely to lead to a decrease in total output, shortages of some consumer goods, and, possibly, to unemployment. In a centrally planned economy full employment would probably be artificially supported, but output would almost certainly fall if existing plant and equipment could not be maintained, while the new level of current consumption would be influenced by government policy. Thus, the maintenance of full employment would ensure that per capita consumption was more evenly spread among the population than in a market economy, but the aggregate level of consumption would fall if an attempt was made to replace producers goods imports by domestic output of similar goods if this were technically feasible. If, however, an economy's reliance on foreign trade is largely restricted to 'extensive' growth-generating capital imports, a cessation of trade would merely restrict the short-term rate of growth of capacities – and, soon, of output – but without affecting existing production processes. Although this line of argument has never been made explicit, there is historical evidence to suggest that the PLA leadership probably thinks in this way. In other words, the technological restructuring of the Albanian economy necessitated by the split with the Soviet Union in 1961 was in some measure due to the economy's inability otherwise to maintain production with the plant and equipment supplied by the Comecon countries. Given that the policy of self-reliance first appeared in Albanian economic discussions following the failure of the Third Five-year Plan (1961–5), it seems possible that the PLA leadership will consider the economy completely self-reliant only when a rate of growth of output equal to the rate of growth of the population is possible in the absence of foreign trade.

The contemporary Albanian economic system and the PLA's development strategy are the product of both history and Stalinist ideology, and it seems reasonable to conclude that, while historical circumstances have fashioned the PLA's approach towards foreign economic policy, on the domestic front the quest for rapid industrialization has been tempered by a desire to produce a society more imbued with Stalin's ideology than his own ever was.

THE ALBANIAN ROAD TO SOCIALISM

The three years 1974–6 were marked by the sharpest divisions on Albanian economic policy since those surrounding the break with the Soviet Union and the intimate alignment with China in 1960–1. As then, the only overt sign in the official press that fundamental issues of policy had been in dispute were the dismissal, arrest, trial, and (in some cases) execution of those PLA and government leaders who had opposed the policies of Enver Hoxha and Mehmet Shehu. The losers, in the field of economic policy, in 1974–6 were the holders of the three principle economic ministries: Abdyl Kellezi, Chairman of the State Planning Commission; Koço Theodhosi, Minister of Industry and Mining; and Kiço Ngjela, Minister of Trade. So clean a sweep of the economic leadership – all were stated to have been dismissed around October 1975 – implied a fundamental divergence of view within the Central Committee of the PLA; the subsequent dismissal of the Minister of Agriculture, Piro Dodbiba, the sole remaining holder of an economic portfolio, early in the following year may not have been associated with that dispute. The background to the dispute was the scaling-down of Chinese aid to and the general under-fulfilment of, the Fifth Five-year Plan (1971–5), contrasting with the over fulfilment of the previous five-year plan.

It was suggested in Chapter 3 that the three purged ministers had argued for a retreat from the Stalinist priority for the fulfilment of ambitious plans for heavy industry in times of economic difficulties, regardless of the adverse implications for other sectors of the economy. They may well have argued that the adoption of this policy during the Third Five-year Plan had led to mass unrest and thus put the leadership of the party in jeopardy. In fact, the fulfilment of the 1971–5 Plan indicators for light industry and consumption, and the more rapid rate of growth of group B production than group A output during 1974–5, indicate that, in practice if not in theory, the Stalinist rules had been at least temporarily abandoned.

None the less, some indication of the previous success of the strategy may be given by the fact that in 1975, when Albania possibly received no foreign aid and had a balance of payments surplus with China – after suffering short-falls on promised aid in 1973 and 1974 – global industrial output nevertheless increased by 4 per cent. On the other hand, since Albania did not expect to be self-sufficient in spare parts (servicing the present level of technology) before 1980, it is unlikely that an annual growth rate of industrial output of 4 per cent could be maintained indefinitely in the absence of foreign aid. Given that global industrial output rose by 8 per cent in 1976, it is likely that Chinese equipment deliveries were resumed, although no concrete data on the state of Sino-Albanian trade up to 1978 are available.

Now that Albania is no longer receiving Chinese aid, it is difficult to predict the likely outcomes for the Albanian economy. If the Albanian authorities decide that the economy should maintain a balance of visible trade even before attaining a satisfactory degree of self-sufficiency in intermediate goods, it is possible that a large part of Albania's trade will be with the developed capitalist economies of Western Europe, and the agreement signed between the Albanian and Greek governments to open a Tirana–Athens air link may have been a first step in this direction. Now that China has lost the status, in the Albanian press, of a socialist economy, any future Albanian requirement for foreign credit would pose the PLA constitutional problems, given the barring of such loans by the existing constitution; and since that constitution was promulgated in 1976, when difficulties over aid from China had already surfaced, it seems highly unlikely that the break in the relationship between Tirana and Peking was initiated on the Albanian side.

It seems reasonable to argue that, without the emphasis placed on development of energy resources and industrial spare-parts production by the PLA's economic Stalinism, the Albanian economy would have fared worse than it did, following the cut-back of Chinese aid in 1975. Considering future possibilities, if Albania has been able to extract sufficient aid from China to complete the metallurgical complex at Elbasan (a complex covering a greater area than Port Douglas), it could then become the first country in Eastern Europe to be free of foreign creditors. On the other hand, such a situation would also imply the lowest level of per capita consumption in Eastern Europe. But, as has earlier been demonstrated, the PLA's approach to consumption is extremely frugal. Indeed, the PLA leadership may have decided that an independent economy growing at a moderate rate, in which the entire population is clothed, fed, and sheltered and women have been freed for the workforce by the ready availability of simple labour-saving devices for the home, represents a reasonable short-term approximation to 'full communism'. If that is the case, and if the Albanian economy can reach this level in the near future, then Stalinist economic ideology will have helped the PLA solve what is arguably the most difficult problem facing a developing economy: the need to alleviate extreme poverty while still 'developing' and not incurring an intolerable burden of foreign debt.

APPENDIX A

PLAN CONSTRUCTION IN THE ALBANIAN INDUSTRIAL ENTERPRISE

The following table shows the major annual plan indicators for a typical Albanian industrial enterprise. The contents of the table are discussed in Chapter 2.

TABLE A1 *Plan construction in the Albanian industrial enterprise*

Parts and major indicators of the plan	Organ that draws up plan	Organ approving plan	Information needed to draw up the plan	Source of information
(1) *Production plan*				
(a) Output mix (in physical units)	Planning branch	Superior organs	Final products, goods in process industrial services and co-operation details	Superior organs and enterprise placing orders
(b) Global output	Planning branch	Superior organs	(1) Output mix (2) Approved wholesale prices (3) Plan for incomplete production and imput requirements	Planning branch Superior organ Shipment co-ordinator*
(c) Cooperation plan	Planning branch	Superior organs	(1) Balance of goods in process (2) Goods in process to be obtained through co-operation	Material technical supply and sales Technology office
(2) *Quantity of Production Plan*	Planning branch	Superior organs		

I	II	III	IV	V
(a) Quantity categories of output	Planning branch		(1) Physical output mix	Planning branch
			(2) Standard and technical conditions	Organs of quality control
			(3) Plan for quality improving technico-organizational measures	Technology office
(b) Intervals for servicing production	Technology office		As for quality plan	Technology office
(3) *Productive Capacity plan*	Planning branch	Superior organs		
(a) Average annual capacity	Planning branch		(1) Data on machines' productive space	Chief mechanic
			(2) Investment and capital construction plan	Chief engineer; Chief mechanic
(b) Machine and productive space loadings	Planning branch		(1) Output mix	Planning branch
			(2) Unit output machine time norms and the planned utilization rate	work Organization branch
(c) Exploitation of productive capacity	Planning branch		(1) Output mix	Planning branch
			(2) Average annual capacity	Planning branch
(4) *Investment and capital construction plan*				

I	II	III	IV	V
(a) Volume and structure of capital investment	Chief engineer	Superior organs	(1) Production plan (2) Average annual capacity (3) Projects and budgets (4) Project prices	Planning branch Chief mechanic Chief mechanic Superior organs
(b) Exploitation of new productive capacity	Chief engineer	Superior organs	(1) Production plan (2) Average annual capacity	Superior organs Planning branch
(c) List of projects	Chief engineer	Superior organs	Technical projects	Chief mechanic
(5) *Labour and wages plan*	Work organization branch	Superior organs		
(a) Group labour productivity	Work organization branch	Superior organs	(1) Plan for technico-organizational measure to increase production (2) Norms for labour time per unit output (3) Plan for revision of norms (4) Number of workers according to skill categories	Work organiztion branch Work organization branch Work organization
(b) Planned number of workers	Work organization branch	Superior organs	(1) Output mix (2) Planned incomplete production (3) Balance of workers' useful work time for the year.	Planning branch Planning branch Work organization branch

I	II	III	IV	V
			(4) Planned percentage realization of work norm	Work organization branch
(c) Supplementary workforce plan	Work organization branch	Superior organs	(1) Anticipated level of work force at the end of the last year	Work organization branch
			(2) Workforce plan for the coming year	
			(3) Planned flow of workforce during coming year	Work organization branch
			(4) Sources of supplementary workforce	Superior organs
(d) Planned number of other categories of workers	Work organization branch	Superior organs	(1) Organized recruitment	Superior organs
			(2) Plan of technico-organizational measures for the minimal use of these categories of workers	Work organization branch
(e) Training of new workers and increase in skill category of existing workers	Work organization branch		(1) Supplementary workforce plan	Work organization branch
			(2) Planned number of workers by shift category	
			(3) Training period of workers	Work organization branch
(f) Wage fund	Work organization branch	Superior organs	(1) Work force by skill category and professions	Work organization branch
			(2) Workers wage rates	Superior organs
			(3) Organized recruitment	Superior organs

I	II	III	IV	V
			(4) Tables of wages for management	Superior organs
			(5) Norms for labour time per unit output and their planned percentage realization	Work organization branch
			(6) Balance of workers' useful time for the year	Work organization branch
(g) Average wages	Work organization branch	Superior organs	(1) Wage fund (planned)	Work organization branch
			(2) Planned number of workers by skill category	Work organization branch
			(3) Planned percentage increase in labour productivity	Work organization branch
			(4) Percentage of increase in labour productivity to be secured by direct merit of workers	Work Organization branch
(6) *Material–technical supply and sale of output*	Supply branch	Superior organs		
(a) Input requirements (excluding electricity)	Supply branch		(1) Output mix	Planning branch
			(2) Planned goods in process	Planning branch
			(3) Norms for unit output raw material requirements	Technology office
			(4) Supporting department plan	Chief mechanic chief technician for energy

I	II	III	IV	V
			(5) Investment and capital construction plan	Chief mechanic
			(6) Input prices	Superior organs
			(7) Plan of measures for the rational use of inputs	Technology office and supply branch
(b) Electrical energy requirements	Chief technician for energy		(1) Planned volume of production	Planning branch
			(2) Norms for energy requirements per unit output	Chief technician
			(3) Work plan of departments and their regime of work	Planning branch
(c) Sales plan	Superior branch	Superior organs	(1) Output mix	Planning branch
			(2) Output prices	Superior organs
			(3) Unsold output and goods in process	Supply branch
(7) *Cost plan*	Planning branch	Superior organs		
(a) Cost of production per unit of output	Planning branch	Superior organs	(1) Norms of input requirements per unit output	Technology office
			(2) Input prices	Superior organs
			(3) Wages per unit output	Work organization branch
			(4) Budget of departmental enterprise expenses	Planning branch
(b) Budget of production expenses	Planning branch	Superior organs	(1) Production plan in money terms	Planning branch

I	II	III	IV	V
			(2) Material technical supply plan in money terms	Planning branch
			(3) Wage fund	Work organization branch
			(4) Depreciation charges	Planning branch
			(5) Budget of other expenses	Planning branch
(c) Absolute and percentage cost reduction plan	Planning branch	Superior organs	(1) Output mix	Planning branch
			(2) Actual cost of products in the base year	Planning branch
			(3) Plan of technico-organizational measures for cost reduction	Management
			(4) Economic outcomes of carrying out the measures for cost reduction	Planning branch
(8) *Technical development plan*		Superior organs		
(a) Plan for new products and the perfection of existing products	Technology office		(1) List of new products and old ones requiring improvement	Planning branch and technology office
			(2) Construction plan for new products	Technology office
			(3) Technological plan for new products	Technology office
			(4) Organizational and input plan for new products	Technology office
			(5) Unit cost of new products	Planning branch

I	II	III	IV	V
(b) Research and development plan	Technology office in conjunction with management		(1) Plan of new production techniques	Technology office
			(2) Plan of ideo-political and technico-organizational measures for the exploitation of internal reserves	Management
(c) Plan of technico-organizational measures for the exploitation of internal reserves	Management	Enterprise	(1) Plan of ideo-political and technico-organizational measures for departments	Departments
			(2) Economic efficiency secured by carrying out measures	Management
			(3) Overall plan of measures for the enterprise	Planning branch
(9) *Financial plan*	Accounting branch	Superior organs		
(a) Balance of income and expenses	Accounting branch	Superior organs	All other indicators of the financial plan	
(b) Profit plan	Accounting branch	Superior organs	(1) Production plan	Planning branch
			(2) Sales plan	Supply branch
			(3) Wholesale prices	Superior organs
			(4) Turnover tax prices	Superior organs
			(5) Percentage retail mark-ups	Superior organs
(c) Plan of working capital norms	Accounting branch	Superior organs	(1) Production plan	Planning branch
			(2) Input requirements norms	Technology office

			(3) Input prices	Superior organs
			(4) Prices of finished products and goods in process	Superior organs
			(5) Cost of production	Planning branch
			(6) Schedules of production cycles	Planning branch
(d) Sources of finance for working capital	Accounting branch	Superior organs	(1) Wage fund	Work Organization branch
			(2) Planned expenses for electrical energy	Chief technician for energy
			(3) Profit	Accounting branch
			(4) Sources from other enterprises	Superior organs
			(5) Budgeting finance	Superior organs
(e) Plan for finance of investments and large undertakings	Accounting branch	Superior organs	(1) Average annual fixed capital situation	Chief mechanic
			(2) Depreciation norms	Superior organs
(f) Sources of finance for investment and large undertakings	Accounting branch	Superior organs	(1) Depreciation fund for investments and large undertakings	Superior organs
			(2) Profit	Superior organs
			(3) Budget	Superior organs
			(4) Bank credit	Superior organs
(g) Depreciation fund plan	Accounting branch	Superior organ	(1) Average annual value of fixed capital	Superior organs
			(2) Depreciation norms	Superior organs
(h) Turnover tax plan	Accounting branch	Superior organ	Same data as for profit plan	Superior organs

APPENDIX B

THE SPECIAL CASE OF COLLECTIVE AGRICULTURE

An interesting example of a change in Albanian system rules is provided by the establishment of a new form of agricultural economic unit. The interest lies largely in the use made of Stalinist ideology in attempting to solve the problem of distinctions of ownership between cooperatives and state farms.

The management of an agricultural cooperative differs from that of a state enterprise – be it industrial or agricultural – in that the principle of one-man management – however much influenced by the local party organs – is replaced by 'collegiality', so that the day-to-day administration of the cooperative is the collective responsibility of a management board comprising the director, one or more deputy directors, and certain senior staff.[1] Whereas the principle of democratic centralism is officially the sole management criterion in state enterprises, in the cooperative it is supplemented by the concept of 'internal cooperativist democracy', whereby the management of the cooperative is elected by the members of the cooperative, with the advice of the local party and state organs, and is accountable to its members.[2]

Up to 1971 cooperative members derived income from a combination of payments in cash and in kind as a labour-day dividend, and from the produce of their household plots.[3] The plot has been diminished several times under PLA pressure in the ten years up to the mid-1970s, on each occasion the government offsetting the income forgone by increases in agricultural procurement prices, reductions in the prices of goods bought by farmers, and, most recently, the payment of state pensions to eligible farm members. The increment in procurement prices was not accompanied by a rise in state-determined retail prices (which overall have slightly fallen), and the difference was subsidized to the extent of 27 million leks in the three years 1967–9[4] and 'hundreds of millions' in the six years 1970–5.[5]

In 1971 the system of collective remuneration was brought in line with practice elsewhere in Eastern Europe by the introduction of monthly advances, aggregating 70–80 per cent of the labour-day dividend, the remainder to be paid at the end of the year to the extent that the plan is fulfilled.[6] More importantly, that year (on 15 July) a new form of collective was introduced: the 'higher-type agricultural cooperative'[7] is an ingenious solution to an ideological problem of some importance to the PLA.

Stalinist ideology requires that the mechanization of collective agriculture be undertaken via state-owned machine and tractor stations

(MTS) because the transfer of capital goods from state to group ownership would represent ideological retrogression. Further, in *Economic Problems of Socialism in the USSR* it is argued that the collective farms would not have sufficient investible funds to ensure that agriculture benefited from technological advances:

What . . . would be the effect of selling the machine and tractor stations to the collective farms as their property? The effect would be to involve the collective farms in heavy loss and to ruin them, to undermine the mechanization of agriculture, and to slow up the development of collective-farm production.[8]

The PLA has never changed its position on this issue, and has always harshly criticized the USSR for abolishing the MTS. Of course, the provision of machinery services was never the sole function of the MTS in the Soviet Union or Albania. In both it was partly responsible for agricultural procurement; it had to assist in the collectivization drive; and, perhaps most important in Albania, it was charged with spreading the party's message among the peasants. Hence, for the PLA the MTS remains an indispensible unit of organization in agriculture.

On the other hand, plan fulfilment has always been a problem in Albanian agriculture, and increased capital investment in the cooperative sector was essential if crop yields were to be raised to a satisfactory level. In 1970, comparing the cooperatives with state farms, food grain yield on the farms was only 85 per cent; cow milk yield, 47 per cent; the level of mechanization, 64 per cent; and the volume of annual investment, 60 per cent.[9] But it is clear from these figures – although the former Minister of Agriculture, Piro Dodiba, did not choose to draw the conclusion – that in grain and milk production the cooperatives were achieving higher levels of output per unit of mechanization and investment than were the state farms.

The ideological considerations just described meant that investment in the cooperatives themselves could take place only on the basis of internal accumulation, short-term state aid, and long-term bank credits; budget grants for investment in machinery had to be confined to the MTS. However, while the new higher-type cooperative of 1971 continues to receive short-term state aid, long-term bank credit has been replaced by direct investment out of the state budget, and the state becomes a part-owner of the cooperative to the extent of its investment in it. In this way the ideological standing of the investment remains unaffected; it is still state property.

The method of remuneration of members of the higher-type cooperative lies between those of ordinary cooperatives and of state farms. Thus, workers in the higher-type cooperatives are paid 90 per cent of their wages, determined by planned norms, fortnightly and the remainder at the end of the year provided the plan has been fulfilled.[10] The difference between this system and that in ordinary cooperatives is that in the latter case payment is based on labour-days, the value of the labour-day depending on output, whereas in the case of the higher-type cooperative a minimum wage is paid regularly and later supplemented according to the fulfilment of the production plan (which is no longer determined internally but, as with state farms, as part of the state plan).[11]

The provision of machinery for the higher-type cooperative provides a further example of ideological ingenuity. Whereas the state farm owns its machinery and the average cooperative is one of several being serviced by an MTS, each higher-type cooperative has the exclusive services of an MTS. Thus, the agricultural machinery remains *de jure* state-owned, but in terms of availability to the cooperative there has been a *de facto* transfer of control. The ultimate aim of the PLA is the conversion of all ordinary cooperatives into higher-type cooperatives and eventually the complete elimination of both group and private ownership. However, for the time being members of higher-type co-operatives are still entitled to a private plot. The prerequisite for transition from ordinary to higher-type cooperative status has been and continues to be 'economic strength'; thus the cooperatives must, in some undefined sense, be ready for ideological advancement.[12] By 1976, higher-type cooperatives occupied 23 per cent of the arable land and produced 25 per cent of the grain, 40 per cent of sunflowers, and more than half the rice and cotton produced by the cooperative sector.[13] No higher-type cooperatives have as yet been transformed into state farms, nor has a clear transition mechanism been defined. As Enver Hoxha put it in 1971:

> Life, the revolutionary practice of our socialist construction, will show us later the other stages through which this process will have to pass. It will indicate the measures that should be taken to gradually eliminate those differences which exist today between these two forms of socialist property.[14]

APPENDIX C

ALBANIAN STATISTICAL SOURCES

Introduction

The quantity of official Albanian statistics published is roughly correlated with Albania's economic position in the socialist world. Thus, it publishes fewer statistics than the relatively developed economies of Eastern Europe but rather more than the underdeveloped economies of Asia. Statistical yearbooks were published annually up to 1965 and appeared biennially between 1967–8 and 1971–2. Since that time, there has only been one statistical publication of note, *30 vjet Shqipëri socialiste* (Tirana, 1974), an *ersatz* yearbook. It is not clear whether further statistical yearbooks will be published in the near future.

The reliability of Albanian statistics cannot be measured directly. However, it is likely that inaccuracies will arise owing to distortion at the enterprise level – a common feature of other Eastern European statistics. It seems much less likely that statistics are deliberately distorted at the central level, for two reasons. First, with respect to the statistics used in this book, there is little evidence of inconsistencies between various sources. Such discrepancies as do occur may be ascribed to rounding errors or changes in methodology. Second, sufficient economic failures have been published to indicate that the reported successes are plausible. In the case of a particularly undesirable outcome – such as the drop in industrial labour productivity noted in Table 3.1 – the datum is not reported and must be calculated indirectly.

For the purposes of most of the statistical analysis in this book it is necessary to convert particular data published at current prices into a constant price series. The relative scarcity of statistics generally precludes any choice between alternative methodologies in the calculation of price indices. Consequently, it has proved necessary, in most cases, to estimate the only index possible. In the Albanian case this is unlikely to be crucial, as almost any index chosen – if the choice were available – would suffer from a defect certain to outweigh all others: namely, that the rapid growth of the Albanian economy since 1945 has been accompanied by a marked change in the composition of aggregates such as global industrial production and gross investment.

The decision to convert all aggregates into 1971 prices has, likewise, been determined by the nature of Albanian statistical publications. Thus, values for global industrial product are generally given in 1956, 1960, 1966, or 1971 prices, since these were years of reforms in industrial wholesale prices. On the other hand, for reasons that are not clear, gross investment has been valued at 1958, 1961, and 1971 prices. For the sake of consistency, then, 1971 prices must be used. The unavoidable problem caused by this constraint is that, where absolute values of a particular variable have not been published, it has been necessary to use growth indices based on a Laspeyres formula, which employs base-year (probably 1956) price weights; i.e.,

$$\frac{p_1 q_0}{p_0 q_0}$$

(*Statistike ekonomike*, Tirana, 1972, p. 148).
Statistical calculation at a level of sophistication encountered in research on other Eastern European economies is clearly not possible. On the other hand, to the extent that the statistical data used in Chapters 3, 4, and 5 have not been in conflict with qualitative expectations, it may be argued that the manipulations required to produce the data in their final form have been justified. The remainder of this appendix is devoted to an outline of the sources and methods used in the preparation of certain tables in the body of the text.

Chapter 3

(a) Table 3.1

The value of global industrial production in 1971 prices is given for 1950, 1955, 1960, and 1970 in *Vjetari statistikor i RPSh 1971–2* (Tirana, 1972), p. 55. The 1973 value is given in *30 vjet Shqipëri socialiste* (Tirana, 1974), p. 55, while the value for 1975 is calculated from 52 per cent increase in global industrial production compared with 1970 (*Rruga e partisë*, no. 12, 1976, p. 11).

To obtain the value of global industrial production in 1963 at 1971 prices a price index must be calculated. This is obtained by dividing the value of global industrial production in 1960 expressed at current prices (*Vjetari statistikor i RPSh 1964*, Tirana, 1964, p. 133) by the evaluation at 1971 prices (*Vjetari statistikor i RPSh 1971–2*, p.55), which yields an index of 11.496. Dividing this into the 1960 prices evaluation of global industrial production in 1963 (*Vjetari statistikor i RPSh 1964*, p.133) yields 3,385 million leks at 1971 prices.

30 vjet Shqipëri socialiste, p.45, gives the number of industrial workers in 1963 and 1973 and an index of industrial labour productivity for 1960, 1970, and 1973 related to 1950 = 100. The data for 1975 are obtained from the increases in industrial labour productivity and global industrial product, during the Fifth Five-year Plan, of 21 and 52 per cent respectively (*Rruga e partisë*, no. 12, 1976, p.11). Because data on the Albanian industrial wage fund have not been published, it is necessary to use productivity data expressed in units of lek per man for the analysis in Chapter 3. However, the Albanian productivity series are probably calculated with reference to the wage bill. For the sources considered thus far this is unimportant, since 1971 prices have been used throughout. On the other hand, the estimate of productivity change for the 1951–5 period, which is cited as 70 per cent (*PPSh Dokumenta kryesore*, vol. II, Tirana, 1972, p. 612), was possibly calculated using 1956 prices. This amount is therefore deflated by a price index of global industrial production and the result divided by 10 to account for the switch from old leks to new leks. The derivation of the index, 12.47, is given below (sources for Table 3.4). The resulting increase of 56 per cent between 1950 and 1955 is then used to calculate the value of industrial labour productivity in 1955.

(b) Table 3.2

The Albanian capital stock is calculated from several sources. A gross investment series is given, in 1971 prices, in *Vjetari statistikor i RPSh 1971–2*, p. 115, and reproduced in Table A2). *30 vjet Shqipëri socialiste* and annual plan reports provide the data for 1973 and 1975, while *Vjetari statistikor 1965* allows the determination of the value for 1963. The labour force data of Table 3.1 are then used to calculate the capital–labour ratio.

TABLE A2 *Gross investment.*
(million leks, 1971 prices)

1938	13	*1951*	396	*1960*	1,065	*1969*	2,052
1945	15	*1952*	543	*1961*	1,112	*1970*	2,207
1946	44	*1953*	536	*1962*	964	*1971*	2,461
1947	136	*1954*	317	*1963*	1,016		
1948	166	*1955*	458	*1964*	1,320		
1948	166	*1956*	500	*1965*	1,617		
1949	158	*1957*	646	*1966*	1,783		
		1958	985	*1967*	1,672		
1950	303	*1959*	1,070	*1968*	1,692		

(c) Table 3.4

M.C. Kaser, 'External Economic Relations', in M.C. Kaser and A. Schnytzer, *The Albanian Economy from 1945 to the 1980 Plan* (Papers in East European Economics, no. 52, St Antony's College, Oxford), p. V–13, gives the value of Albanian exports and imports, at current prices, over the relevant period. A former employee of the Albanian Planning Commission (Mrs A. Palacios, St Antony's College, Oxford) has stated that the value of Albanian imports is expressed in domestic prices. Since no official Albanian source gives a contradictory impression, it is assumed that a simple price index may be used to convert the trade data into 1971 prices. The index chosen is calculated on the basis of data relating to gross industrial production because the analysis in Chapter 3 and 4 is concerned only with the surplus of imports over exports as a measure of foreign capital inflow. The content of the surplus may thus be reasonably assumed to comprise predominantly industrial goods. Finally, it is assumed that an index relating 1956 to 1971 prices may be applied to the pre-1956 data.

Similarly, the values of global industrial production for 1960 in 1971 and 1956 prices, given in, respectively, Kaser, 'External Economic Relations' and *Vjetari statistikor i RSPh 1965* (Tirana, 1965), p. 126, are used to calculate a deflator of 12.47. *Vjetari statistikor i RPSh 1965,* p. 127, expresses 1960 global industrial production in 1960 prices, facilitating the calculation of an index linking 1960 prices with 1971 prices. The value of the index is 0.08699.

Chapter 4

(a) Table 4.3

The ratio of foreign aid to gross investment is calculated on the basis of Table 3.4 and the investment series in *Vjetari statistikor i RPSh 1971–2*, p. 115. This source is used in conjunction with *Rruga e partisë*, no. 12, 1976, p. 11, which states that gross investment for the years 1971–5 was 50 per cent greater than it had been in the 1966–70 period, to calculate the value of A/I for 1971–5.

(b) Econometric estimations

The econometric estimates given in Chapter 4 were all obtained using the 'Fakad' program on the Oxford University computer. The program gives all R^2 values corrected for degrees of freedom. The values of Y_{It-1} used in equation (6) were calculated on the basis of the price indices noted above and are presented in Table A3. The values of A follow from Table 3.4, while the investment series is from *Vjetari statistikor i RPSh 1971–2.*

TABLE A3 *Lagged global industrial product* (million leks at 1971 prices)

1960	*1961*	*1962*	*1963*	*1964*	*1965*
281	195	195	214	259	225

For the regression of incremental output–capital ratios on foreign aid, the value of net material product for the relevant years was calculated on the basis of the 1970 estimate in 1971 prices given by Kaser and Schnytzer, *The Albanian Economy*, pp. 1-21, and the indices of annual growth of net material product were found in *30 vjet Shqipëri socialiste*, p. 183; *Ekonomia popullore*, no. 6, 1972, p. 119; *Vjetari statistikor i RPSh 1969–70*, p. 105; *Vjetari statistikor i RPSh 1965*, p. 345; and *Anuari statistikor i RPSh 1960* (Tirana, 1960), p. 276. The calculated values of $\Delta Y/I$ are shown in Table A4 (1971 prices).

TABLE A4 *Incremental output–capital ratio*

1956	0.050	*1961*	0.218	*1966*	0.295
1957	0.534	*1962*	0.218	*1967*	0.330
1958	0.176	*1963*	0.383	*1968*	0.112
1959	0.462	*1964*	0.183	*1969*	0.301
1960	0.077	*1965*	0.002	*1970*	0.242

TABLE A5 *Components of per capita consumption* (million new leks)

	B	*0.5D*	*0.915R*	*A*	*X*	*C*	*P*
1950	98	74	512	655	170	1.1	1.22
1955	208	97	1,049	893	249	1.5	1.39
1956	249	76	1,132	714	305	1.2	1.42
1957	306	78	1,386	893	316	1.5	1.46
1958	497	110	1,818	655	284	1.1	1.51
1959	582	106	2,059	1,072	274	1.8	1.56
1960	600	105	2,061	655	262	1.1	1.62
1961	622	120	2,105	714	219	1.2	1.66
1962	655	135	2,157	774	211	1.3	1.71
1963	713	139	2,324	714	208	1.2	1.76
1964	746	140	2,456	834	220	1.4	1.81
1965	767	146	2,524	953	240	1.6	1.87
1966	812	140	2,731	1,250	260	2.1	1.91
1967	837	151	2,913	1,429	277	2.4	1.96
1968	918	168	3,170	1,489	301	2.5	2.02
1969	1,064	217	3,490	1,548	332	2.6	2.08
1970	1,210	238	3,551	1,667	338	2.8	2.14
1971	1,346	255	4,035	1,369	384	2.3	2.19
1973	1,516	293	4,458	1,846	424	3.1	2.3

B = budgetary expenditure on social and cultural sectors
D = budgetary defence expenditure
R = socialist sector retail turnover
A = autoconsumption
X = private sector retail turnover
G = index of bread grain production (in physical units)
P = population (in millions)

A is calculated by weighting the 1970 value by the index of grain production. Consumption is then obtained as

$$B + 0.5D + 0.915R + A + X$$

and the population data are used to obtain the index of per capita consumption shown in the text.

The following sources were used:

(1) *30 vjet Shqipëri socialiste*, pp. 21, 115, 177, 190;
(2) *Anuari statistikor i RPSh 1959* (Tirana, 1959), pp. 27, 94–5, 159, 179;
(3) *Vjetari statistikor i RPSh 1965*, pp. 63, 198–9, 289, 348;
(4) *Vjetari statistikor i RPSh 1969–70*, pp. 23, 73, 98, 106;
(5) *Anuari statistikor i RPSh 1960*, pp. 53, 139, 223, 277.

(b) Table 5.7

Personal disposable income was calculated as

$$0.915R + X + \text{(annual change in personal savings)}.$$

The savings data are cited in the above sources, as follows;

(1) p. 195;
(2) p. 185;
(3) p. 350;
(4) p. 110;
(5) p. 284.

NOTES

PREFACE

1. For an analysis of more recent events see A. Schnytzer, 'The Impact of the Sino-Albanian Split on the Albania Economy', *Assessment: Part 1 – Country Studies, 1980* (US Government Printing Office, Washington, 1981), pp. 619–49.

CHAPTER 1

1. One may feel confident of this even though (1) the global output indices may contain increasing duplication as 'backward and forward linkages' increased with industrialization; and (2) the spread of the money economy may have resulted in an increasing coverage of output – and certainly of consumption as represented by retail sales – in the statistics.
2. This weakness is particularly pronounced in A. Logoreci, *The Albanians*, London, 1977.
3. The party being the Communist Party of Albania (CPA) or the Party of Labour of Albania (PLA).
4. W. Brus, *The Market in a Socialist Economy*. London, 1972.
5. The term 'planning system' is here, and subsequently, used as shorthand for 'the system of planning and management of the economy', comprising not only the rules and institutions for the formulation of plans but also those for plan implementation.
6. *History of the Party of Labour of Albania* (hereafter *History*). Tirana, 1971, p.27.
7. R. Marmullaku, *Albania and the Albanians*. London, 1975, p. 45.
8. The official interpretation of these struggles is given in *History*, pp. 46–60, 73–85.
9. *History*, p. 88.
10. E. Hoxha, *Selected Works*, vol. 1. Tirana, 1974, p. 42.
11. Ibid., p. 41.
12. S. Skendi, Albania. New York, 1956, p. 136.
13. Ibid.
14. Hoxha, op. cit., p. 91.
15. Ibid.
16. N.C. Pano, *The People's Republic of Albania*. Baltimore, 1968, p. 66. The quotations that follow are to be found from pp. 67 to 85.
17. Hoxha, op. cit., p. 64.
18. Ibid., p. 65.
19. Pano, op. cit., p. 87.
20. Marmullaku, op. cit., p. 37.
21. Ibid.
22. *UN, ECE, Economic Survey of Europe in 1960*. Geneva, 1961, p. VI–1.

23. Ibid., p. VI–3.
24. Ibid., p. VI–4.
25. J.V. Stalin, *Economic Problems of Socialism in the USSR*. Peking, 1972, p. 45.

CHAPTER 2

1. J.V. Stalin, *Economic Problems of Socialism in the USSR*. Peking, 1972, p. 7.
2. Ibid., p. 21.
3. Ibid., p. 19.
4. E. Hoxha, *Selected Works,* vol. 1. Tirana, 1974, p. 669.
5. Ibid., p. 674.
6. *History of the Party of Labour of Albania* (hereafter, *History*). Tirana, 1971, p. 381.
7. J. Elezi, *Bazat e shtetit dhe të së drejtës së RPSh* (The Basis of the State and Law in the PRA). Tirana, 1959, p. 330.
8. *History*, p. 531.
9. N.C. Pano, *The People's Republic of Albania*. Baltimore, 1968, p. 175.
10. *Zëri i popullit*, 26 December 1965.
11. *Zëri i popullit*, 12 January 1966. The 8.8 per cent was doubtless an unusual case (though not abnormal in the West among dockers) since, on average, absence in Eastern Europe is 4 per cent of work-day potential.
12. *PPSh Dokumenta kryesore* (Major Documents of the PLA), vol. IV. Tirana, 1972, pp. 539–57.
13. *Zëri i popullit*, 3 November 1965.
14. Ibid.
15. *Ekonomia popullore*, no. 1, 1966, pp. 3–12.
16. A. Backa, 'The Simplification and Improvement of the Planning Methodology', *Ekonomia popullore*, no. 2, 1966, pp. 14–27. The following discussion draws heavily on this article.
17. *History*, pp. 568–9.
18. Ibid., p. 569.
19. *Përmbledhëse e përgjithshme e legjislacionit në fuqi te R.P.Sh* (1945–1971) (General Collection of Legislation in Force in PRA). Tirana, 1971, pp. 89 *et seq.*
20. E. Hoxha, *Speeches 1967–8*. Tirana, 1969. The following four extracts are from pp. 31, 33–4, 50–1, and 55.
21. *Zëri i popullit*, 22 February 1968.
22. *PPSh Dokumenta kryesore*, vol. 5, pp. 253–7. Throughout this book, the word 'cadre' is used to describe any person with specialist technological or political training. The term thus encompasses both 'reds' and 'experts'. It is used interchangeably with the term 'employee' in Chapter 5 below.
23. *Zëri i popullit*, 29 April 1967.
24. *Zëri i popullit*, 24 March 1968.
25. *Rruga e partisë* (the Journal of the PLA), no. 3, 1968, p. 13.
26. *Zëri i popullit*, 4 May 1968.
27. *Rruga e partisë*, no. 5, 1968, p. 27.
28. *Zëri i popullit*, 15 May 1968.
29. *Information Bulletin of the Central Committee of the PLA*, no. 4, 1968, pp. 5–6. The next four extracts are from pp. 11, 19, 23–4, and 26.
30. H. Banja, J. Fullani, and H. Papajorgji, *Probleme te organizimit e te drejtimit te ekonomisë popullore në R.P.Sh.* (Problems of Organizing and Managing

the People's Economy in the PRA). Tirana, 1973, p. 326.
31. It should be noted that the planning branch of the enterprise referred to in the table is a management organ, not to be confused with the workers' planning commissions mentioned earlier.
32. *Probleme ekonomike*, no. 2, 1973, p. 39.
33. *Përmbledhëse e pergjithshme e legislacionit në fuqi në R.P.Sh.* (1945–1971) (A General Collection of Legislation in Force in the PRA). Tirana, 1971, p. 426.
34. Interview material, Durrës, April 1977.
35. Enver Hoxha, *Report Submitted to the Seventh Congress of the PLA*. Tirana, 1976, p. 70.
36. Ibid., p. 68.

CHAPTER 3

1. J.V. Stalin, *Economic Problems of Socialism in the USSR*. Peking, 1972, pp. 40–1.
2. Ibid., p. 68.
3. *Ekonomia politike e socializmit* (The Political Economy of Socialism), vol. 1. Tirana, 1975, p. 182.
4. *Ekonomia politike e socializmit*, vol. 3. Tirana, 1976, p. 65.
5. P.J.D. Wiles, *The Political Economy of Communism*. Oxford, 1964, p. 273.
6. Ibid., p. 283.
7. 'The planning and Finance of Investment in the Soviet Union and Eastern Europe', in *UN Economic Survey of Europe in 1955*. Geneva, 1956, p. 200.
8. Ibid.
9. An explanation of the fall in the ratio from 1960 to 1963 is suggested below.
10. *History of the Party of Labour of Albania* (hereafter *History*). Tirana, 1971, p. 328.
11. E. Hoxha, *Selected Works*, vol. 1. Tirana, 1974, p. 452.
12. Assuming that the trade deficit is an adequate indicator of the scale of aid.
13. M.C. Kaser, 'Trade and Aid in the Albanian Economy', in Joint Economic Committee, US Congress, *East European Economies post-Helsinki*. Washington, 1977.
14. Hoxha, op. cit., p. 744.
15. E. Hoxha, *The Khrushchevites: Memoirs*. Tirana, 1980, pp. 67–72.
16. Ibid., pp. 68–9.
17. Hoxha, *Selected Works*, vol. 2. Tirana, 1975, p. 381.
18. B. Bardhoshi, *Probleme të planifikimit dhe të zhvillimit të ekonomisë së planifikuar në R.P.Sh.* (Problems of Planning and Development of the Planned Economy in the People's Republic of Albania). Tirana, 1965, p. 145.
19. *Vjetari statistikor i RPSh 1965*. Tirana, 1965, p. 128.
20. *PPSh Dokumenta Kryesore* (Major Document of the PLA) (hereafter *D.K.*), vol. III. Tirana, 1972, pp. 549–50.
21. Ibid.
22. P.J.D. Wiles, *Communist International Economics*. Oxford, 1968, p. 400.
23. Hoxha, *The Khrushchevites*, pp. 81–2.
24. Kaser, op. cit.
25. A list of construction projects completed between 1946 and 1970 is given in *Vvjetari Statistikor i RPSh 1971–72*, Tirana, 1972, pp. 119–25.
26. N.C. Pano, *The People's Republic of Albania*. Baltimore, 1968, p. 137.

27. *D.K.*, vol. III, pp. 558–9.
28. *History*, p. 491.
29. Ibid., p. 503.
30. The decline in production in contemporary Czechoslovakia administered a shock which was one of the factors behind the institution of economic reform throughout Comecon from 1964 onward.
31. *D.K.*, vol. V, pp. 207–8. Annual fluctuations in farm output owing to weather of course reduce the significance of such comparisons of agricultural production in isolated years.
32. M. Papajorgji and E. Luçi, *Mbi disa probleme të perqendrimit, specializimit e kooperimit në industri* (On Some Problems of Concentration, Specialization and Cooperation in Industry). Tirana, 1968, p. 143.
33. *Rruga e partisë*, no. 11, 1965, pp. 68–75, provides a discussion of this problem.
34. *Zëri i popullit*, 19 April 1968.
35. *Zëri i popullit*, 22 February 1969.
36. Ibid.
37. *Probleme ekonomike*, no. 3, 1974, pp. 3–20.
38. *Vjetari statistikor i RPSh, 1967–8* and *1971–2.*
39. *30 vjet Shqipëri socialiste* (30 Years of Socialist Albania). (hereafter *30 vjet*). Tirana, 1974, p. 65.
40. *Ekonomia e industrisë në RPSh* (The Economics of Industry of Socialism), vol. II. Tirana, 1972, p. 337.
41. M. Shehu, *Report on the Fifth Five-year Plan, (1971–75)*. Tirana, 1971, p. 18.
42. E. Hoxha, *Report Submitted to the Sixth Congress of the PLA*. Tirana, 1971, p. 91.
43. *30 vjet* p. 64.
44. Ibid., pp. 55–6.
45. *Probleme ekonomike*, no. 1, 1975, pp. 4 and 112; no. 1, 1976, p. 5.
46. E. Hoxha, *Reflections on China* (2 vols). Tirana, 1979.
47. Ibid., vol. 1, p. 755.
48. *Probleme ekonomike*, no. 1, 1973, p. 137; no. 1, 1974, pp. 6, 8; no. 1, 1975, p. 6.
49. Kaser, op cit.
50. *Vjetari Statistikor i RPSh 1971–72.*

CHAPTER 4

1. See also M.C. Kaser, 'Trade and Aid in the Albanian Economy', *East European Economies Post-Helsinki*, Washington, 1977.
2. K. Griffin, 'Foreign Capital, Domestic Savings and Economic Development', *Bulletin of the Institute of Economics and Statistics*, May 1970.
3. P.J.D. Wiles, *Communist International Economics*, Oxford, 1968, p. 402, values income from the base at around $10 million against a visible deficit of $40 million at that time.
4. *Vjetari statistikor i RPSh 1971–72*, (Statistical Yearbook of the PRA). Tirana, 1972, p. 115.
5. C.S. Voivodas, 'Exports, Foreign Capital Inflow and Economic Growth', *Journal of International Economics*, vol. 3, no. 4, 1973, pp. 337–49.
6. Not only is gross investment only an approximation to the increment of the

capital stock, but also we are here relating the increment of the *total* capital stock to the increment of *material* product only.

7. This variable was introduced to improve the poor fit obtained in its absence for the 1961–6 period:

$$\underset{}{\Delta I} = \underset{(1.70)}{3.43\, \Delta A} + \underset{(59)}{64} \quad R^2 = 0.382$$

The incorporation of Y_{It-1} into the other three equations neither improved the fit significantly nor altered the coefficient *a*. The possible reasons for this are considered below.

8. North Korean development is discussed in J. Robinsons, 'Korean Miracle', *Monthly Review*, January 1966. However, since the mid-1960s North Korea has borrowed heavily in the West.
9. J.V. Stalin, *Economic Problems of Socialism in the USSR*. Peking, 1972, pp. 40–1.
10. Wiles, op.cit., p. 402.
11. *The Times*, 27 July 1977.
12. M.C. Kaser, *Comecon: Integration Problems of the Planned Economies*, 2nd ed. London, 1967, p. 106.
13. *The Times*, 19 July 1977.
14. *Kushtëtuta e Republikës Popullore Socialiste te Shqiperisë.* Tirana, 1976, pp. 20–1.
15. Kaser, 'Trade and Aid in the Albanian Economy'.

CHAPTER 5

1. J.V. Stalin, *Economic Problems of Socialism in the USSR*. Peking, 1972, pp. 40–1.
2. *Ekonomia politike e socializmit*, vol. 1. Tirana, 1975, pp. 180–1.
3. *Vjetari statistikor i RPSh.* Tirana, 1965, p. 294.
4. This is the ratio calculated by A.S. Becker for the Soviet Union in his *Soviet National Income 1958–1964*. Berkeley and Los Angeles, 1969, p. 332.
5. *Statistike ekonomike*. Tirana, 1972, p. 434.
6. The percentage of the population living in towns rose from 20.5 per cent in 1950 to 33.9 per cent in 1973: *30 vjet Shqipëri socialiste*. Tirana, 1974, p. 22.
7. *A New Victory of the Policy of the PLA in Uplift of the General Well-being of the People*. Tirana, 1976, pp. 23–4.
8. *Vjetari statistikor i RPSh 1965,* pp. 306–7.
9. E. Hoxha, *Selected Works*, vol. 2. Tirana, 1975, p. 369.
10. Ibid., pp. 366–7.
11. Ibid., p. 367.
12. Ibid.
13. *Ekonomia politike e socializmit*, p. 16.
14. Stalin, op.cit., pp. 24–9.
15. Ibid., p. 27.
16. Z. Lika, *Disa cështje mbi përmirësimin e mëtejshem të planifikimit dhe të shpërblimit sipas punës si kushtit për forcimin e drejtimit të ekonominë socialiste* (Several Questions on the Further Improvement of Planning and Distribution according to Work as Conditions for Strengthening the Management of the Socialist Economy). Tirana, 1964, p. 150.

17. *Information Bulletin of the Central Committee of the PLA*, no. 3, 1967, pp. 10–11.
18. Interview material, July 1975.
19. *Information Bulletin of the Central Committee of the PLA*, no. 3, 1967, p. 11.
20. Lika, op. cit., p. 159.
21. E. Sejko, H. Papajorgji, J. Fullani, O. Murati, and G. Mara, *Bazat e organizimit socialist të punës dhe drejtimit* (The Basis of Socialist Organization of Work and Management), vol II. Tirana, 1973, p. 279.
22. *A New Victory*, op. cit., p. 16.
23. Ibid., p. 7.
24. Ibid., p. 16.
25. E.E. Anderson, The Growth of Income, Consumer Discretion, and the Accumulation of Stocks in Socialist Economies', *Papers in East European Economics*, no. 45. Centre for Soviet and East European Studies, St Anthony's College, Oxford, (mimeographed).
26. It is the build-up of unsaleable stocks of some consumer goods that precludes the interpretation of the rise in savings as evidence of 'thwarted consumption', in the sense that nothing was available on which this income could have been spent.
27. *Vjetari statistikor i RPSh 1969 dhe 1970.* Tirana, 1970, p. 110.
28. Ibid.
29. *Probleme ekonomike*, no. 2, 1979, p. 32.
30. *Information Bulletin of the Central Committee of the PLA*, no 1, 1970, p. 5.

APPENDIX B

1. A. Kallapodhi, N. Dumani, and K. Kote, *Bazat e ekonomise dhe organizimit të bujqesisë socialiste* (The Basis of the Economics and Organization of Socialist Agriculture). Tirana, 1971, p. 523.
2. Ibid., pp. 520–1.
3. *Financat e ndërmarrjeve dhe degëve të ekonomisë popullore* (The Finance of Enterprises and Branches of the People's Economy). Tirana, 1972), Part II, p. 13.
4. Ibid., p. 116.
5. *Albania Today* , no. 1, 1976, p. 20
6. *Financat e ndërmarrjeve*, p. 13.
7. *Gazete zyrtare*, no. 8, 1971.
8. J.V. Stalin, *Economic Problems of Socialism in the USSR*, Peking, 1972, p. 95.
9. P. Dodbiba, in *Albania Today*, no. 5, 1974, pp. 24–9.
10. Ibid.
11. *Financat e ndermarrjeve* , p. 117.
12. E. Hoxha, *Report to the Seventh Congress of the PLA*, Tirana, 1976., p. 54.
13. Ibid., p. 55.
14. E. Hoxha, *Report to the Sixth Congress of the PLA*, Tirana, 1971, p. 84.

BIBLIOGRAPHY

PRIMARY SOURCES

Articles

Backa, A., 'The Simplification and Improvement of the Planning Methodology', *Ekonomia popullore*, no. 2, 1966, pp. 14–27.

Ballco, I.P., 'For a Thorough Knowledge and Creative Application of Methods of Planning the National Economy', *Ekonomia popullore*, no. 4. 1968, pp. 3–13.

Bardhoshi, B., 'Strengthening the Scientific Character of Planning – an Important Basis for the Correct Execution of the Party's Economic Policy', *Rruga e partisë*, no. 8, 1976, pp. 36–47.

Jakubini, I., 'For a Better Understanding of the Simplification of Statistics', *Ekonomia popullore*, no. 3, 1967, pp. 16–33.

Books

Anuari statistikor i RPSh 1959 (Statistical Yearbook of the PRA 1959). Tirana, 1959.

Anuari statistikor i RPSh 1960 (Statistical Yearbook of the PRA 1960). Tirana, 1960.

Banja, H., Fullani, J. and Papajorgji, H., *Probleme të organizimit e të drejtimit të ekonomisë popullorë në RPSh* (Problems of Organizing and Managing the People's Economy in the PRA). Tirana, 1973.

Bardhoshi, B., *Probleme të planifikimit dhe të zhvillimit të ekonomise së planifikuar ne RPSh* (Problems of Planning and Development of the Planned Economy in PRA). Tirana, 1965).

Bocari, N.E., *Shtetëzimi i mjetëve të prodhimit në RPSh* (Nationalization of the Means of Production in the PRA). Tirana, 1973.

Bollano, P., *Probleme të drejtimit të prodhimit socialist* (Problems of Managing Socialist Production). Tirana, 1972.

Ekonomia e industrisë ne RPSh (The Economics of Industry of Socialism). Tirana, 1972.

Ekonomia politike e socializmit (The Political Economy of Socialism). Tirana, 1976.

Elezi, J., *Bazat e shtetit dhe të së drejtës së RPSh* (The Basis of State Law in the P.R.A.). Tirana, 1959.

Financat e ndërmarrjeve dhe degëve te ekonomisë popullore (The Finance of Enterprises and Branches of the People's Economy). Tirana, 1972.

Gijiriti, D., *Mbi mirëqenien e punonjësve të qytetit e të fshatit* (On the Well-being of Workers of Town and Country), Tirana, 1973.

History of the Party of Labour of Albania. Tirana, 1971.

Hoxha, Enver, *Report to the Sixth Congress of the PLA*. Tirana, 1971.
—, *Report Submitted to the Seventh Congress of the PLA*. Tirana, 1976.
—, *Selected Works*, vol. 1. Tirana, 1974.
—, *Selected Works*, vol. 2. Tirana, 1975.
—, *Speeches 1967–8*. Tirana, 1969.
Kallapodhi A., Dumani, N. and Kote, K., *Bazat e ekonomisë dhe organizimit të bujqesisë socialiste* (The Basis of the Economics and Organization of Socialist Agriculture). Tirana, 1971.
Kedi, V. and Luci, E., *Programini linear në problemat ekonomike* (Linear Programming in Economic Problems). Tirana, 1970.
Kushtetuta e Republikës Popullore Socialiste të Shqipërisë (Constitution of the People's Socialist Republic of Albania). Tirana, 1976.
Letër e hapur e kometetit qendror të RPSh (Open Letter of the Central Committee of the PLA). Tirana, 1975.
Lika, Z., *Disa cështje mbi përmirësimin e mëtejshëm të planifikimit dhe të shperblimit sipas punës si kushtit për forcimin e drejtimit të ekonominë socialiste* (Several Questions on the Further Improvement of Planning and Distribution according to Work as Conditions for Strengthening the Management of the Socialist Economy). Tirana, 1964.
A New Victory of the Policy of the PLA in Uplift of the General Wellbeing of the People. Tirana, 1976.
Pano, N.C., *The People's Republic of Albania*. Baltimore, 1968.
Papajorgji, M. and Luçi, E., *Mbi disa probleme të përqendrimit, specializimit e kooperimit në industri* (On Some Problems of Concentration, Specialization and Cooperation in Industry). Tirana, 1968.
Përmbledhëse e përgjithshme e legjislacionit në fuqi në RPSh [1945–1971] (A General Collection of Legislation in Force in the PRA [1945–71]). Tirana, 1971.
PPSh Dokumenta kryesore (Major Documents of the PLA). Tirana, 1974.
Sejko, E., Papajorqji, H. Fullani, J., Murati, O. and Mara, G., *Bazat e organizimit socialist të punës dhe drejtimit* (The Basis of a Socialist Organization of Work and Management). Tirana, 1973.
Shehu, M., *Report on the Fifth Five-year Plan (1971–75)*. Tirana, 1971.
—, Report to the Seventh Congress of the PLA. Tirana, 1976.
Stalin, J.V., *Economic Problems of Socialism in the USSR*. Peking, 1972. *Statistike ekonomike* (Economic Statistics). Tirana, 1972.
30 vjet Shqipëri socialiste (30 Years of Socialist Albania). Tirana, 1974.
Vjetari statistikor i RPSh 1964 (Statistical Yearbook of the PRA 1964). Tirana, 1964.
Vjetari statistikor i RPSh 1965 (Statistical Yearbook of the PRA 1965). Tirana, 1965.
Vjerari statistikor i RPSh 1967–8 (Statistical Yearbook of the PRA

1967–8) Tirana, 1968.

Vjetari statistikor i RPSh 1969–70 (Statistical Yearbook of the PRA 1969–70). Tirana, 1970.

Vjetari statistikor i RPSh 1971–2 (Statistical Yearbook of the PRA 1971–2). Tirana, 1972.

Xhaja, B. and Murati, O., *Probleme të ekonomisë dhe të organizimit në industrinë mekanike* (Problems of Economics and Organization in the Engineering Industry). Tirana, 1974.

Xhuvani, P., Gorica, I. Sejko, E. and Bollano, P., *Organizimi, planifikimi i veprimtarisë ekonomiko-prodhuese të ndërmarrjeve industriale* (The Organization and Planning of the Economico-productive Activity of Industrial Enterprises). Tirana, 1973.

Newspapers and Journals

Albania Today
Bashkimi
Ekonomia popullore
Gazeta zyrtare
Information Bulletin of the Central Committee of the Party of Labour of Albania
Probleme ekonomike
Puna
Rruga e partisë
Zëri i popullit

SECONDARY SOURCES

Articles

Anderson, E.E., 'The Growth of Income, Consumer Discretion, and the Accumulation of Stocks in Socialist Economies', *Papers in East European Economics,* no. 45. Centre for Soviet and East European Studies, St. Antony's College, Oxford (mimeographed).

Domar, E.D., 'Depreciation Replacement and Growth', *Economic Journal,* March 1953, pp. 3–10.

Griffin, K., 'Foreign Capital, Domestic Savings and Economic Development', *Bulletin of the Institute of Economics and Statistics*, May 1970. pp. 99–112.

Kaser, M.C., 'Albania', in H. Hohmann, M. Kaser and K. Thalheim, *The New Economic Systems of Eastern Europe*. London, 1976, pp. 251–73.

–, 'Trade and Aid in the Albanian Economy', in Joint Economic Committee, US Congress, *East European Economies post-Helsinki*, Washington, 1977, pp. 1325–40.

Koopmans, T.C. and Montias, J.M., 'On the Description and Comparison of Economic Systems', in A. Eckstein (ed.), *Comparison of Economic Systems*. Berkeley, 1971, pp. 27–78.

'The Planning and Finance of Investment in the Soviet Union and

Eastern Europe', *UN Economic Survey of Europe in 1955*. Geneva, 1956, pp. 198–217.

Robinson, J., 'Korean Miracle', *Monthly Review,* January 1966, pp. 541–9.

Voivodas, C.S., 'Exports, Foreign Capital Inflow and Economic Growth', *Journal of International Economics,* vol. 3, no. 4, 1973, pp. 337–49.

Ward, I.D.S., 'Introduction to a Study of Comparative Economic Systems' (Mimeographed notes). Melbourne, 1973.

Books

Becker, A.S., *Soviet National Income 1958–1964*. Berkeley and Los Angeles, 1969.

Eckstein, A. (ed.), *Comparison of Economic Systems*. Berkeley, 1971.

Griffiths, W.E., *Albania and the Sino-Soviet Rift*. Cambridge, Mass., 1963.

Hohmann, H., Kasar, M., and Thalheim, K., *The New Economic Systems of Eastern Europe*. London, 1976.

Joint Economic Committee, US Congress, *East European Economies post-Helsinki*. Washington, 1977.

Kaser, M.C., *Comecon: Integration Problems of the Planned Economies,* 2nd ed. London, 1967.

Kaser, M.C. and Zielinkski, J., *Planning in East Europe*. London, 1970.

Logoreci, A., *The Albanians*, London, 1977.

Marmullaku, R., *Albania and the Albanians*. London, 1975.

Prior, F.L., *The Communist Foreign Trade System*. London, 1963.

Skendi, S., *Albania*. New York, 1956.

Thomas, J.I., *Education for Communism*. Stanford, 1969.

UN Economic Survey of Europe in 1960. Geneva, 1961.

Wiles, P.J.D., *Communist International Economics*. Oxford, 1968.

–, *Economic Institutions Compared*. Oxford, 1977.

–, *The Political Economy of Communism*. Oxford, 1964.

INDEX